Translation: A Very Short Introduction

VERY SHORT INTRODUCTIONS are for anyone wanting a stimulating and accessible way into a new subject. They are written by experts, and have been translated into more than 40 different languages.

The series began in 1995, and now covers a wide variety of topics in every discipline. The VSI library now contains over 450 volumes—a Very Short Introduction to everything from Psychology and Philosophy of Science to American History and Relativity—and continues to grow in every subject area.

Very Short Introductions available now:

Available soon:

For more information visit our website

www.oup.com/vsi/

Matthew Reynolds

TRANSLATION

A Very Short Introduction

OXFORD
UNIVERSITY PRESS

OXFORD
UNIVERSITY PRESS

Great Clarendon Street, Oxford, OX2 6DP,
United Kingdom

Oxford University Press is a department of the University of Oxford.
It furthers the University's objective of excellence in research, scholarship,
and education by publishing worldwide. Oxford is a registered trade mark of
Oxford University Press in the UK and in certain other countries

First edition published in 2016

Impression: 5

Published in the United States of America by Oxford University Press
198 Madison Avenue, New York, NY 10016, United States of America

British Library Cataloguing in Publication Data
Data available

Library of Congress Control Number: 2016939849

ISBN 978–0–19–871211–4

Printed and bound by
CPI Group (UK) Ltd, Croydon, CR0 4YY

Contents

Acknowledgements

This little book maps a vast landscape and I am grateful to scholars who helped me through areas where my footing was unsure or pointed out landmarks I might otherwise have missed: Tania Demetriou, Mona Baker, Valentina Gosetti, James Hadley, Xiaofan Amy Li, and Mohamed-Salah Omri. I owe particular thanks to Adriana Jacobs and an anonymous assessor, both of whom read the manuscript and suggested corrections and improvements, and to Jenny Nugee, Joy Mellor, Gillian Northcott Liles and others at OUP for transforming the text into a book. The thinking that went into these pages was nourished by the collaborative spark and warmth of the research collective Oxford Comparative Criticism and Translation (OCCT); I am grateful to The Oxford Research Centre in the Humanities, St Anne's College, and Maria Ferreras Willetts for supporting it.

List of illustrations

Chapter 1
Crossing languages

What is translation?

You are in school. On the whiteboard there are words in a foreign language. Your task is to understand their meaning and transfer it into English. The teacher glowers. The clock ticks. Sunlight slants across the room. Mistakes will be punished.

The test is called 'translation'.

You are the 17th-century poet John Dryden. You have been brought up reading as much Latin as English; the writer you most love is Virgil. You translate and imitate Latin poems as often as you compose your own. But your own poems also include an element of translation because Latin and English words and phrases run together in your imagination as you write. Now, in the 1690s, towards the end of your career, you are translating the complete works of Virgil for publication in a big, expensive volume. You want to give new readers a sense of Virgil's brilliance. You also want to dignify English literature by raising it to his level.

That is another instance of translation.

You are an Italian teenager. You are chatting to some friends. As is often the case, pretty much everywhere around the world, the group is multilingual. You say, 'Ma dai, non ci credo!' Your French friend says, 'Quoi?' You say, 'I not believe it.' The words that you've come out with don't have the same nuance as what you said in Italian, and they are not in perfect Standard English either. But your friend still gets the gist.

Is that translation?

You are in hospital. Gravely, the doctor informs you that you have suffered a TIA. 'That means,' she says, 'a transient ischaemic attack.' Oh?'—you respond, enquiringly. She explains: 'the blood supply to your brain was interrupted but then restored. It's like a temporary little stroke.'

What about that?—Is that translation?

How about what happens whenever anyone says anything? Or what is happening now, as you read this text that I have written? Don't we all know a slightly different range of words from one another, and use them slightly differently? Don't we all, to that extent, speak a different language? Isn't this obvious from the frequency with which we misunderstand each other, getting the wrong end of the stick? (What end of the stick did you just get?—to some readers that idiom will mean 'misunderstand' and to others 'be short-changed'.)

If that is so, then translation must happen when we speak or write or read or hear the language that we think of as our own just as much as languages we call foreign.

But in that case why do we need the word translation at all? If translation is no different from communication in general why do we generally assume that it is?

These brief, everyday instances have begun to show how nebulous the field of translation is, and how tricky it can be to think about.

They also suggest a way for us to start. There is no point trying to insist on our own clear, rigid meaning for the word—no point trying to say, for instance, that translation only really happens between different standard national languages like Japanese and French and not between dialects or different varieties of the same language. There is no point asserting that a 'true translation' must catch the 'spirit' of the source text, or taking the opposite view (like Vladimir Nabokov) that it should aim at expository precision above all. If you take that sort of stance, you shut out the complexities that make the subject interesting: you stake a claim but don't explore the territory.

Instead, we need to look at the range of ways of doing things with words that can be thought of as translation, from what seem typical instances like Dryden's *Virgil* or the classroom test to less obvious ones like the doctor's explanation. We need to see how it matters whether we call something translation or not, and work out where to draw what sort of distinction. We need a map, one that registers the many features of the landscape: contours, boundaries, and conceptual marshy areas. To begin to sketch it, let's look now at some more extended examples from the territory of translation in different historical moments and places around the globe.

The no man's land between languages

Japanese and Chinese overlap. The spoken languages are different, but the written forms have much in common. The reason is that the Chinese developed writing first, and when Japanese needed to be written down scribes simply borrowed the Chinese characters. During the Tokugawa Shogunate (1603–1868) this state of affairs led to an activity that was both like and unlike the usual Western ideas of 'translation'. Texts written in Classical Chinese were made intelligible by a process known as '漢文訓読', *kanbun-kundoku*, which means, roughly, 'Chinese text, Japanese reading'. Faced with a piece of Chinese writing, a scholar would add little marks to show how the characters would be arranged in Japanese: this made the text intelligible to someone who could not speak Chinese but had been trained in *kanbun-kundoku*. A further step was to rewrite the characters in Japanese order, and add signs for pronunciation: a text like this could be understood by most literate Japanese people.

Kanbun-kundoku does not transfer meaning between two languages. Rather, it creates a sort of no-man's land that readers of one language can enter to make sense of writing in another. 'This is quite different from how translation functions in the West!' we might exclaim. But is it? This morning I received a spam email in German and put a sentence into Google Translate. The result: 'in Germany alone there are around 25 million signs that help to make the road and to make safe for all road users'. The individual words are correct Standard English but the idiom and grammar have a German shape. Here, as with *kanbun-kundoku*, the writing is neither completely in one language nor completely in another.

Google Translate is of course a fairly recent development. People sometimes make fun of it for producing this sort of translation which feels strange or incomplete. But in fact lots of translation is like this, and always has been. Think of the last time you had a conversation with someone whose first language was not your own. Just like our Italian teenager from a moment ago, their use of your language was probably not perfect—nor perhaps your use of theirs. Translations done in a rush, or else done very carefully as word-for-word cribs, can have a similar feel. There is a technical term—'translationese'—for this way of putting words together which falls between two tongues.

'Translationese' is often used to voice a criticism: 'this isn't a successful translation—it's translationese'. But the language of translations is almost always at least a bit different from the language of texts that have not been translated. This strangeness can be a source of poetry. In Ezra Pound's collection of poems *Cathay* the arrangement of the English words is modelled on Chinese and Japanese writing:

> Blue, blue is the grass about the river
> And the willows have overfilled the close garden.

Another famous example is the King James Bible whose cadences, influenced by the Hebrew and Greek from which it was translated, seemed challengingly foreign when it was published in 1611. Yet, over centuries of repetition, the King James Bible's translationese came to seem familiar to many English speakers. Some even judged it to be an ideal of English style.

Across history, and around the world, linguistic oddities created by translation have been absorbed into the texture of national languages. This is what happened to thousands of Latin words that were drawn into English during the 16th century. There was cross-pollination between German and the classical languages at the start of the 19th century, and between Japanese and European languages at its end. Similar processes are happening all around the globe right now as English is used for cross-cultural communication by people who know it as their second or third or fourth language, and who re-shape it to suit their location and their needs.

Here is the first discovery for our map. Translation does not simply jump from one language to another. It also 'crosses languages' in the sense of blending them, as you might cross a bulldog with a borzoi, or two varieties of rose.

Diplomatic translation

In England, in the 16th-century court of Queen Elizabeth, letters arrived from the Ottoman Sultan Murad III. They had been composed in Turkish and then re-written by the Sultan's translator, his *dragoman*, in Italian, a language which Elizabeth and her courtiers could understand.

Murad assumed that he was the grandest ruler in the world, and he thought of Elizabeth as a minor potentate: his letter claimed that she had 'demonstrated her subservience and devotion' (*izhar-i ubudiyet ve ihlas*). The *dragoman* realized that Elizabeth might not be very pleased to know this. His most important aim in translating was not to transfer meaning between languages. If he did that, he risked causing an international crisis or losing his head. For the *dragoman*, translation was crucially a matter of keeping open a channel of communication, of greasing the wheels of diplomacy. So he wrote that Elizabeth had demonstrated, not 'subservience', but *sincera amicizia* ('sincere friendship').

This aspect of translation—mediation, the avoidance of conflict—is crucial in diplomatic negotiation. Figure 1 shows another instance: the translator and diplomat Amédée Jaubert (with the open hand) is advising the Persian envoy, Mirza Mohammed Reza Qazvini, who is about to meet Napoleon to form an alliance. The same consideration comes into play whenever mutually acceptable phrasing is negotiated among the twenty-four official languages of the European Union. In the charged environment of a war zone, lives can depend on an interpreter's tact in choosing words.

In fact, every act of translation negotiates between two powers. The aim of conveying what a speaker or source text is saying has to be tempered by an awareness of what the listener or reader is prepared to take on board. So our second orientation point is this: all translation involves diplomacy.

Crowd translation

In China, in the first few centuries of what people in the West call 'AD' or 'the common era', Buddhist holy texts were being translated. Typically no written source was present. A monk, who might have

1. François Mulard, *The Persian Envoy Mohammed Reza Qazvini, Finkenstein Castle, 27 April 1807.*

travelled from India, and who knew a Sutra by heart, would recite it bit by bit, perhaps in Sanskrit, perhaps in one of several possible intermediary languages. An assembly of as many as a thousand linguistic and religious experts would listen, ponder, and debate until they reached an interpretation of each phrase; a scribe would then record the result in Chinese brushwork characters.

It is easy to see that translation in this case is more complicated than it is often thought to be. The monk's words are translated, not only between languages, but from speech to writing. With the change of medium, a great deal shifts. Sound and intonation are lost; and visual form is gained. Some ambiguities disappear while others flower (this happens in all languages, including English: try reading out 'she hit me with a scull': would a listener hear 'scull' or 'skull'?) In fact, translation often crosses media as well as languages: subtitles are a modern, everyday example.

The Chinese Buddhist scenario also seems unusual because translation is done by a crowd rather than a single translator. But this too is less rare than you might think. It took forty-seven scholars working in teams to create the 1611 King James Bible. In 1680, a famous translation of Ovid's *Epistles* was done by John Dryden and 'several hands'. More recently, translations of Joyce into French and Proust into English have shared out the work between several translators. Websites offer quick translation services which are typically done by translators working in trios or pairs. Crowd-sourcing platforms allow translations to be done by large numbers of volunteers; and any translator can draw on shared knowledge by posting a question to an online forum. Machine translation software also draws on the labour of crowds. It searches many previous translations in order to find the best fit for whatever phrase you ask it to translate.

Crowd translation is helpful simply for coping with large volumes of text. But it also shows us something crucial about the sort of interpretation that translators engage in. The reason why the King

James Bible was translated by committee was not just that it was big: after all, the Bible (or large portions of it), had been translated by individuals before, such as St Jerome, Luther, and Tyndale. The translators needed to arrive at a version that was in harmony with the community they were translating for—the recently established Church of England—and the faith that they communally held. The translators brought their Church's assumptions with them to the work of translation. They translated their source text in line with meanings that their faith told them it must have. Modern machine translation also does its best to produce text that will be acceptable to its users.

In fact, all translators feel some pressure from the community of readers for whom they are doing their work. And all translators arrive at their interpretations in dialogue with other people. The English poet Alexander Pope had pretty good Greek, but when he set about translating Homer's *Iliad* in the early 18th century he was not on his own. He had Greek commentaries to refer to, and translations that had already been done in English, Latin, and French—and of course he had dictionaries. Translators always draw on more than one source text. Even when the scene of translation consists of just one person with a pen, paper, and the book that is being translated, or even when it is just one person translating orally for another, that person's linguistic knowledge arises from lots of other texts and other conversations. And then his or her idea of the translation's purpose will be influenced by the expectations of the person or people it is for. In both these senses (this is our third key discovery) every translation is a crowd translation.

Let me count the ways

When Elizabeth Barrett Browning published her celebrated sonnet 'How do I love thee? Let me count the ways', she pretended it was a translation, one of the 'Sonnets from the Portuguese' that were concealed at the back of her book *Poems*

(1850). She did this out of shyness, because she wanted nobody to guess how personal the poems were. But the title also pointed to the idea that love-sonnets are always in a sense translations because they derive from a trans-linguistic tradition and cannot help re-using material from elsewhere. The first sonnets in English, in the 16th century, were translations of Petrarch by Sir Thomas Wyatt, and the language of love draws thoughts and images from many languages. Poetry is often said to be untranslatable. In fact, translation is at the root of much poetry, and at the heart of what might—at a casual glance—seem like separate national literary traditions.

In these opening pages we have already discovered some perhaps unexpected truths. Translation mixes languages. Translation always involves diplomacy. All translation is crowd translation. We are beginning to see that translation can be done in a variety of ways—but only beginning. Let me (very quickly) count the ways of doing things with language that are commonly thought of as translation.

Translation can seem to turn one written or printed text into another: perhaps this is the most common idea of it. But translation actually makes one text out of several, for (as we saw with Pope) translators inevitably draw on previous linguistic encounters. It can transform written texts into spoken ones, for instance if you translate while reading aloud; and it can make spoken text written, as in the Chinese Sutra translations. It can transpose one spoken utterance into another, as in oral interpreting; and turn recorded speech into different recorded speech (as in dubbing)—or into celluloid or digital subtitles. And it can turn digital text into more digital text, as when your browser takes you to a foreign website and asks, 'Translate this page?'

Translation can move between sign language and spoken language, between pictograms and alphabetic words, and between print and digital multimedia formats. It can set to work on religious books; on poems, novels, and plays; on technical manuals, political speeches, diplomatic negotiations, lawbooks, scientific articles, jokes, insults, ancient inscriptions, declarations of war, and everyday conversation.

Translation can cross languages that have much in common—for example, English and French—and languages that are very distant—like English and Malay; it can span languages that share the same script system (Japanese and Korean) and those that don't (Japanese and Arabic or German); it can go between dialects (or between a dialect and a language) or between different words of the same language, as when our doctor a few moments ago translated 'Transient Ischaemic Attack' into 'like a temporary little stroke'.

Translation can be done by one person, or several, or hundreds—or by machine. It can be a matter of life and death, as in a war zone; or an ordinary part of everyday existence in a multilingual community.

All these instances belong in and around the territory of translation. They all use words to stand in for other words. But there are also large differences between them, and they happen in varied terrains. If we are to pinpoint them on our map, we need to explore how translation relates to other kinds of re-wording.

Chapter 2
Definitions

Translating 'translation'

The name for the Japanese practice of manipulating Chinese characters, which I described in Chapter 1, *kanbun-kundoku*, means something a bit similar to what an English speaker usually means by the word 'translation'—but not very. Such divergences appear again and again in different cultures around the world: every language has its own terms which relate to 'translation' but never completely equate to it. There is no exact translation of 'translation'.

In the ancient Chinese assemblies, the key figures each had their own distinctive titles. The monk who recited and interpreted the sutra was called *zhǔyì* ('主譯'), a term which the Chinese scholar Martha Cheung translates as 'presiding translator', even though he was not in fact exactly a translator because he did not have to know Chinese. A *dùyǔ* ('度語'), literally a 'word-measurer', or a *chuányǔ*, ('傳語'), literally a 'word-transmitter', brought the recitation and explanations of the *zhǔyì* across into Chinese speech. A *bǐshòu* ('筆受'), literally 'received by brush', composed the written version. So the overall process that an English speaker might be tempted to call translation was experienced by its participants as a concatenation of different activities. It must have been a bit like the communal work of cutting and lifting and joining that might go into the construction of a bridge; or of acting, directing, camera-work, and post-production that together make up the shooting of a film.

In the Igbo language of south-eastern Nigeria, there are two words that seem close to 'translation', but they have distinctive connotations:

> *Tapia* comes from the roots *ta*, 'tell, narrate', and *pia*, 'destruction, break [it] up' with the overall sense of 'deconstruct it and tell it (in a different form)'. *Kowa* has a similar meaning, deriving from *ko*, 'narrate, talk about' and *wa*, 'break in pieces'. In Igbo translation is an activity that stresses the viability of the communication as narration, allowing for decomposition and a change in form rather than one-to-one reconstruction.
>
> (Maria Tymoczko, *Enlarging Translation, Empowering Translators*)

In Malay, which is spoken across Malaysia, Indonesia, Singapore, and Brunei, there is a spread of terms that both approximate to 'translation' and depart from it. *Tarjama*, the closest modern translation of 'translate', is used to mean something more like 'explain' or 'clarify'. Other words point to different ways of crossing languages: *terkutip* is close to 'quoted'; *dituturkan* emphasizes the element of re-arrangement; *terkarang* is more like 'newly written' or 'composed'.

In ancient Rome, the words that almost meant 'translation' had a chewy tang of metaphor. The most common were *vertere*, the root of the modern English 'version', whose dominant meanings were 'to set spinning', or 'to turn over ground by digging', and *convertere*, the root of 'convert', which primarily meant 'turn upside-down' and was often used of changes of direction in military manoeuvres. Then there was *exponere*, 'to open'; *explicare*, 'to unfold'; *exprimere*, 'to squeeze'; *reddere*, 'to restore'; and *mutare*, to 'change' or 'metamorphose'.

There were also the words that—when late Latin itself mutated into the romance languages Italian, Spanish, Portuguese, Romanian, and French—became the core terms for talking about translation: *interpretari*, to 'explain' or 'interpret'; *transferre*, 'to carry from one place to another'; and *traducere*, 'to bring across'. It is *transferre*, in its noun form *translatio*, that was itself brought across to become the English word 'translation'.

Yet still, even when the word 'translation' was thoroughly settled into the English language, its meaning would not stay fixed to translation between languages. The 16th-century author John Lyly talks of 'translating' trees—that is transplanting them. The New Testament of the Bible, in the King James version, tells us that Enoch, the father of Methuselah, was so devout that God 'translated' him directly to heaven. In modern biology, 'translation' signifies a process by which proteins are synthesized in cells, while 'translational science' enables discoveries to be put to practical use.

A copy of the *Financial Times*, I noticed in the newsagent, carried the headline: 'Lost in translation: the pitfalls of interpreting Fed policy' where 'translation' stands for the difficulty of making economic predictions on the basis of veiled hints from people in power. The hundredth edition of *Crockford's Clerical Directory* (2007) tells me that Trevor Huddleston, previously Bishop of Stepney, was 'translated' to become Bishop of Mauritius. Probably the best known use of 'translation' to mean something other than translation between languages happens in Shakespeare's *A Midsummer Night's Dream*, where Bottom the weaver is partially transformed into an ass. His friend Quince exclaims:

> Bless thee, Bottom, bless thee!
Thou art translated.

> (Act 3, Scene 1, 118–19)

Here, 'translated' mainly means 'physically metamorphosed'. But it also points to translation between languages and its sometimes strange results. Shakespeare had read about metamorphoses in a translation of Ovid by Arthur Golding, a work that is in many ways wonderful but also a bit odd to read—verbose and rather ponderous. Perhaps Golding's donkey-trot verse rhythms helped Shakespeare come up with the idea of translation into an ass. But Shakespeare was certainly also thinking of the sort of translation that happens within languages. Bottom is translated into an ass because the word 'bottom' can be translated into 'arse'.

There are simple and complex reasons why there is no exact translation of 'translation'. The simple reason is that there is no exact translation of any word. As we will discover in Chapter 3, different languages can never be brought into point-for-point alignment. The word 'translation' is a bit different from the Italian *traduzione*, and very different from *kanbun-kundoku*, just as 'bread' is a bit different from *pane* and more different from the Japanese 'パン' (*pan*). But translation is an especially rich instance of this general truth. This is the complex reason. Because the activities we can call 'translation' are so varied, the word 'translation' keeps having to stretch or shrink to fit them. It keeps on being 'translated', in the Bottom-like sense of shifting shape and meaning. When that happens, other words crowd in to jostle 'translation' and claim parts of the territory.

Other words

Consider 'interpreting', in the sense of oral interpreting between speakers at conferences or in legal discussion. Is this a subset of translation? Or a related but different activity? The title of the famous Scuola Superiore per Interpreti e Traduttori (School of Advanced Study for Interpreters and Translators') in Trieste suggests the second view, but at the end of Chapter 1 I presented oral interpreting as a type of translation and you probably were not shocked. Does a word-for-word 'crib' made by a student count as a translation? Or not quite? What about a 'literal', like the close

15

translations-and-explanations of Homer written by the classicist Donald Carne-Ross for the poet Christopher Logue to use as the basis for his poetic 'version' of the *Iliad*, *War Music*? We might think the 'literal' isn't fully a translation because it isn't really readable on its own as an English text. On the other hand, it might be the 'version' that seems to be not exactly a 'translation' because it is too thoroughly made over into English: it departs from the source and brings in new material.

Subtitling and dubbing look straightforwardly like types of translation—until you realize that they both involve extra, technical aspects such as timing and lip-synching that go beyond what translation is usually thought to be. Or take website localization, which is the process by which multinational companies adapt their websites to suit different markets. This includes linguistic translation alongside other changes to design, content, bandwidth requirements, and so on. Is this a very comprehensive sort of translation? Or is it translation plus other, different processes?

'Translation' has always had a complicated relationship with other words for re-writing, re-arrangement, and explanation. One vivid instance occurred in the 16th century when the introduction of printing to Europe had meant that books were suddenly much more easily and cheaply available than before: reading became possible for masses of new people. Many translations were printed to meet the demand. During the Reformation, the Bible, translated into the European vernacular languages by Luther, Tyndale, Brucioli, Lempereur, and others, could be circulated widely. Because, to believers, fidelity in Bible translation was of ultimate importance, and because printing made it easy to compare translations with the source texts and with one another, questions about what sort of thing a translation was—how accurate, how inventive—were asked with new urgency. In England, people reached for other words to help map the field: 'metaphrase', 'paraphrase', 'imitation'.

In 1680, after 150-odd years of controversy, the great poet and translator John Dryden summed up the debate:

> All translation I suppose may be reduced to these three heads.
>
> First, that of metaphrase, or turning an author word by word, and line by line, from one language into another. Thus, or near this manner, was Horace his *Art of Poetry* translated by Ben Johnson. The second way is that of paraphrase, or translation with latitude, where the author is kept in view by the translator, so as never to be lost, but his words are not so strictly followed as his sense, and that too is admitted to be amplified, but not altered. Such is Mr. Waller's translation of Virgils Fourth *Aeneid*. The third way is that of imitation, where the translator (if now he has not lost that name) assumes the liberty not only to vary from the words and sense, but to forsake them both as he sees occasion; and taking only some general hints from the original, to run division on the ground-work as he pleases. Such is Mr. Cowley's practice in turning two Odes of Pindar, and one of Horace, into English.
>
> (John Dryden, 'Preface' to *Ovid's Epistles*)

Between Dryden's time and ours, the terms of his discussion have all shifted. We would now say 'word-for-word' or 'very literal' translation instead of 'metaphrase'. 'Paraphrase' now generally means translation within a language rather than between languages. 'Version' is now the usual word for what Dryden meant by 'imitation'. Nonetheless, the passage has continued to be very influential: it is much reprinted in anthologies of translation theory, and 'Dryden's tripartite definition of translation' is still taken to be a helpful map of the field.

But what's really interesting is that Dryden couldn't make his definition fit even his own translations. When he thought about it in the abstract, he felt that, though the field of translation was too varied for one word to cover, three might do the trick: 'metaphrase, paraphrase, imitation'. But then, when he turned to the translations that he himself had written, he found that none of those words was quite right. His translations of satires from the Latin poets Juvenal and Persius were, he said, 'betwixt a paraphrase and imitation'. And his greatest work, the translation of Virgil's *Aeneid*, was 'betwixt the two Extreams' of 'Paraphrase' and 'Metaphrase'.

Like all the words that don't quite mean 'translation' in other languages, like all the competing terms in English, and like the fluidity of the word 'translation' itself, Dryden's definition shows the impossibility of pinning translation down. Language is complex, and translations relate to their sources, their translators, and their readers in a multitude of ways. It's turning out that our map is going to have to be like a weather map, re-arranging itself with shifting temperatures, humidities, and winds. What you mean when you call a text 'a translation' will depend on several factors which I will explore further in the chapters to come: your historical moment and political situation, the genre of the text you are talking about, its context and purpose, the features of it that seem to you most important. This is, finally, why there is no exact translation of 'translation'. Instead, the word 'translation' takes its place in a cluster of words for re-stating and re-writing: paraphrase, interpreting, *kanbun-kundoku, exprimere, tarjama*, and the others, all overlapping, blending, or clashing like clouds in a stormy sky.

Translation creates languages

Still, for all this malleability, this shape-shifting translationality of the word 'translation', it can seem hard to get away from the idea that there is such a thing as 'translation in the true sense of the word'. This idea projects a picture in which translation takes something called 'meaning', and transfers it out of one thing called 'a language' into another thing called 'a language'. I will name this picture, 'Translation Rigidly Conceived'.

I will return to the question of 'meaning' in Chapter 3. For now, I want to explore the things called 'languages'.

Imagine that you bump into someone you know. You might, depending on who you are and what the situation is, say 'hello' or 'hi' or 'morning' or 'greetings' or 'wotcha' or 'how're you doing?' or 'hey' or 'awrite' or 'yo' or 'eyup' or 'g'day' or 'ciao' or 'salut' or 'bonjour' or 'coucou'. Each of these words means roughly the same as the others; each, then, is a rough translation of the others, in the fluid sense of 'translation' that we discovered earlier in this chapter. Still, most people are likely to think that 'hi' isn't really a translation of 'hello', whereas 'bonjour' is. After all, 'bonjour' is French and 'hello' is English: they are in different languages. And translation in the true sense of the word works across the barrier between languages.

But where exactly is this barrier?

Jacques Derrida wrote a celebrated essay entitled 'Des tours de Babel', pointing out that proper nouns like 'Babel' belong equally to different languages, including French and English, and arguing that it was therefore impossible to establish a complete distinction between them. He might just as well have focused on all sorts of words that are shared between what we think of as different languages, often with minor shifts of spelling and pronunciation. Look at all the words I have used in this paragraph so far that have almost identical counterparts in French: 'identique', 'paragraphe', 'nombre', 'prononciation', 'mineur', 'langage', 'distinction', 'complète', 'etablir', 'impossible', 'différent', 'Babel', 'noms', 'propres', 'entitulés', 'essai', 'célébré'.

Of course the spelling and pronunication have some slight differences, but how much of a barrier are they? Everyone has their own accent and vocal timbre, and speakers from different regions of England may sound as strange to one another as to someone from France. As for spelling, rules have only become established in Europe over the last 300 years or so, under the pressure of printing and formal modes of written communication like school essays and government reports. People's actual spelling (when uncorrected by computer) varies widely and we might perfectly well come across 'paragraphe', 'prononciation', 'langage', and 'essai' in a piece of English writing alongside 'distinction' and 'impossible'. The variant spellings may be incorrect according to the currently accepted rulebooks; but that needn't stop them being used and understood by English speakers.

Of course there are not the same overlaps between English and more distant languages such as Russian, Zulu, Bengali, or Mandarin. But those languages have their own continuities with adjacent ones (respectively, Polish, Xhosa, Assamese, Cantonese), which have other overlaps in turn. Languages are not separated from each other like islands in a sea. They are more like the undulations of a desert, a continuum in which some kinds of usage can gather into something like a dune that might look different from the dunes around it but in fact shades off into them through infinite shifts and variations.

There are distinctions within languages too. Going back to our array of greetings, I myself am less likely to say 'yo' (too youthful) or 'eyup' (too Yorkshire) than 'salut' or 'ciao', even though those last two words appear on the foreign side of an English–French or English–Italian dictionary. Both sorts of boundary—within languages and between them—are changeable, not so much barriers as habits and tactics of expression. In the continual multiplayer game of everyday communication, language users can adopt whatever words and ways of arranging them work best in the situation they are in. It's even possible I might bring myself to utter 'yo' or 'eyup' in the right ironic or jovial circumstances, just as a French speaker might, if it suited her, say 'ciao' or 'hola' or 'hello'.

Given all this possible variety, how do people ever understand each other? The answer is that we are very good at gauging and obeying shared expectations about how to use our words. We speak differently in the office and the pub, to children and to adults, at a funeral and at a hen party; we write differently in an

20

Instant Messaging (IM) exchange, a PowerPoint presentation, and a novel. In many circumstances these expectations are strongly regulated. Training to be a doctor, say, or a lawyer, includes learning a particular set of words, together with rules for how they should be employed. This book that you are reading has to obey the conventions of formal language use that are required by OUP and other academic publishers. School-teaching, allied with dictionaries, grammar books, and social attitudes, imposes a wider sort of regulation: this gives rise to the idea that there is a correct, standard form of a language as a whole. We have already touched on standardization in connection with spelling, but it regulates other areas too. The standard language authorities tell you which words belong to your language and which don't, and what are the correct ways of putting them together. They are the reason why, if you are a speaker of Standard English, you probably believe you shouldn't never use a double negative.

Behind the obvious influence of schools, dictionaries, and so on lie political and economic interests. States typically promote the standardization of language. Hence the saying, 'a language is a dialect with an army and a navy'. Law-giving and tax-collecting are so much easier when everyone speaks and writes in a similar way. Language is also an important part of group identity, so promoting a uniform language, and getting people to feel attached to it, builds patriotism.

The idea of 'Translation Rigidly Conceived' relies on the standardization of language too. You can't think of yourself as taking meaning out of one language and putting it into another unless you have a sure sense of each language's boundaries, vocabulary, and rules. In fact, it turns out that 'Translation Rigidly Conceived' needs standard languages so badly that, when it doesn't find them ready-made, it joins in the process of creating them.

After the violent breakup of Yugoslavia in the early 1990s, the fragments of the former country needed to establish themselves as separate nation-states. Each therefore wanted its own language. The trouble was that the languages spoken by Bosnians, Croatians, and Serbs were mutually comprehensible, and the boundaries between them had not yet been set up. But the Dayton Peace Accord of 1995, which established the framework for peace between the three groups, had to be written in what counted as three separate languages (plus English). Louise Askew, a member of the Language Service of the NATO-led multinational Stabilisation Force (SFOR), explains how translators rose to the challenge:

> Politically, SFOR language policy, like that of all the international organizations in Bosnia, fed into the divisive ethnic politics in the country by providing documentation and translations in three very similar language versions. Linguistically, too, because much of the translated documentation would go into the public domain, members of the various language services had a hand in moulding the three standards, especially the Bosnian one, about which there are ongoing debates in linguistic circles as to what exactly constitutes the standard. The various orthographies, dictionaries and grammars for Bosnian do not always agree, so there was always much discussion in the SFOR HQ Language Service on what could actually be included in a Bosnian version as against the Croatian or Serbian.

The treaty was a work of linguistic as well as territorial partition. The Dayton Accord is a particularly stark instance. But whenever anyone presents an act of rewording as a 'translation' they promote the idea that they are translating between separate languages. Otherwise—the assumption goes—why would you need a translation? All speakers of Corsican also speak French, so when a book is translated from French into Corsican it does not allow more people to read the book, but it does strengthen the idea that Corsican is a separate language. When the 2008 Basque novel *Bilbao–New York–Bilbao* by Kirmen Uribe is translated simultaneously into Castilian Spanish, Galician, and Catalan a similar point is made. Back in 1844, when William Barnes translated his *Poems in the Dorset Dialect* into 'the dialect which is chosen as national speech' he made the opposite assertion to the same end, putting standard English on a level with the Dorsetshire language which was usually called a 'dialect'. And when, in 1700, John Dryden modernized parts of *The Canterbury Tales*—or, as he put it, 'translated Chaucer into English'—he advanced his own claim to be writing a civilized English worth the name, quite different from the undeveloped medium that Chaucer had to work in.

This is how translation joins in the creation of languages. We will discover in Chapter 6 that it can help to uncreate them too.

Is all communication translation?

We have seen that the idea of 'Translation Rigidly Conceived' defines just one, specially regulated, kind of translation, while translation in the larger sense (I call this 'translationality') spans many other varieties of transmission that take place as much within languages as it does between them. It is time to revisit the question with which we began: is every act of communication an act of translation?

George Steiner took this view in his celebrated book *After Babel* (1975). 'Translation', he declared, 'is formally and pragmatically implicit in *every* act of communication...To understand is to decipher. To hear significance is to translate.' In short: '*human communication equals translation*'. As evidence, he quotes passages from a series of literary works from across the last 500 years: Shakespeare's *Cymbeline*, Jane Austen's *Sense and Sensibility*, a sonnet by Dante Gabriel Rossetti, and Noël Coward's *Private Lives*. He points out how much interpretation the modern, English-speaking reader has to do in order to make sense of them.

Take the following few lines from a soliloquy in *Cymbeline*:

> …that most venerable man, which I
> Did call my father, was I know not where
> When I was stamp'd.

The most obvious strangenesses are the pronoun 'which', instead of the modern English 'who', and the verb form 'I did call', instead of 'I called' or 'I used to call'. In both these cases Shakespeare strikes us rather as Chaucer struck Dryden. Making sense of his words involves knowing how to translate them into a newer idiom: we translate 'which' into 'who', and so on.

Something similar goes on as we think about 'venerable' and 'stamp'd'. Both already had their dominant modern meanings of 'elderly' and 'put your foot down heavily'. But other meanings are likely to have been nearer the surface. 'Venerable' had more of the sense of to be 'venerated' or 'revered' than it does these days, while the idea of imprinting an image on a coin would have been more prominent in 'stamp'd'. So here, too, translation plays a part in developing a full understanding of the words. But it is a smaller and more fluid part than with the first two instances we looked at. We can't simply say 'venerable' means 'X' in the way we can say 'which' means 'who'.

And what about all the other words whose meanings in Shakespeare's writing are not significantly different from their meanings today—'I', 'know', 'where', 'not', 'when', 'was', 'call', 'father'? Of course I *could* choose to translate them into other English words, just as I could choose to translate them into a foreign language. I could explain to myself that a 'father' is a male parent, or that 'I' is a pronoun one uses when speaking of oneself, but why would I? 'I' and 'know' and 'where' and 'not' and 'when' and 'was' and 'call' and 'father' are all familiar to me already. I don't need to read them in translation.

The only way it would make sense to say that understanding these sorts of words is a form of 'translation' would be if there were some secret language in the mind that absolutely all words had to be translated into. On this view, what we call 'meaning' would itself be a kind of language, so that when you understand a word you translate it into 'meaning'. But, if understanding is really a process of translating how would you then understand the 'meaning'? You would have to translate it in its turn. And so on. And on. The structure is endlessly recursive. The reason why communication does not 'equal translation' is simple. You can understand by just knowing the words.

In fact, the relation between thought and language is very complex. Sometimes we think in the words of the languages we know. Sometimes we have the impression of engaging in ordered thought without using any words at all. Sometimes we are prey to emotions which feel a long way from language. Sometimes an idea just pops up. You might still choose the word 'translation' to talk about the action of moving back and forth between language and these variously inchoate processes. But it is important to see that, if you do so, you are speaking metaphorically. Translation in this case does not mean 'using words for other words'.

Steiner's examples end up showing something interestingly different from what he wants them to prove. Translation is not the same as communication. Instead, it is *part of* communication. We reach for translation when we encounter an obstruction to understanding, when we realize that the words that confront us are not entirely within our grasp. This matters because it reveals how fragmented the linguistic environment we inhabit actually is.

As we saw in the last section, the idea of 'Translation Rigidly Conceived' helps to maintain the view that there are separate languages: these are usually official languages supported by political States. If 'translation' is something that only happens between these languages, then it follows that people who have the same official language don't need translation because they can all understand each other without it. But in fact people use language in all sorts of different ways, and there is always scope for misunderstanding.

You can simply not get what someone means and ask them to rephrase (i.e. translate). You might lack the relevant expertise: just now by the coffee machine a colleague said, 'So he bought up the company and IPO'd it' and I had to ask him to translate (it turns out that to 'IPO' means 'to float on the stock market').

You might have a different regional or social identity: the first time one of my kids told me he had had 'a sick evening' it took translation to make me realize he was OK ('sick' is a youth word for what people my age used to call 'cool' or 'wicked'). Or you might be divided by class and political commitment: one person's 'scab' ('strike-breaker') is another's 'hardworking employee'.

This is why it matters to see these linguistic stress-points as translation. Like the idea of 'Translation Rigidly Conceived', translation in the larger sense has the paradoxical effect of drawing attention to divisions in the act of crossing them. It helps us to see, and to respect, the differences between us. The child who writes 'I done it' in a piece of schoolwork doesn't need correcting. He needs help translating.

Chapter 3
Words, contexts, and purposes

Does translation translate the meanings of words?

Take the English word 'house'. If you look it up in a bilingual dictionary it seems easy to translate. In German you can say *Haus*, in French *maison*, in Italian *casa*, in modern Greek *σπίτι*, in Mandarin Chinese '房子' (*fángzi*). There are houses in lots of places around the world, and words for them in very many languages. All these words can be explained with the same rough definition: 'a building for human habitation'. A linguist would say that they share the same 'propositional meaning'.

Now take the word 'scone', in the sense of the English pastry made from flour and egg and typically eaten with clotted cream and jam as a posh treat, accompanied by tea. Look this word up in a German dictionary and you find, not so much a translation, as a description: *weicher, oft zum Tee gegessener kleiner Kuchen* ('a soft little cake, often eaten for tea'). Other dictionaries offer something similar, though more concise: *petit pain au lait* ('small milk roll'); *foccaccina da tè* ('little tea bread'); *είδος γλυκίσματος* ('a form of confectionery'), followed by two words that might stand equally for cookie or bun (*βούτημα, κουλουράκι*); '烤餅' (*kăo bĭng*—'baked biscuits').

Scones are more specific to English culture than houses are, so other languages don't have ready-made words with the same propositional meaning. It takes some effort to find the right phrase to stand in. Often it will seem easier simply to reproduce the English word and explain its meaning in a note or leave it to be deduced from the context. When Greeks speak of English scones they are more likely to say σκον ('skon') than εἶδος γλυκίσματος; and the Chinese too can use a transliterated form of the word, '司康饼' (*sī-kāng-bǐng*). This is how all sorts of terms for culture-specific items (or 'realia', to use the jargon term) have been adopted into many languages. Often they are kinds of food and drink: 'spaghetti', 'curry', 'moussaka', 'camembert', 'whisky', 'limoncello'. But not always: 'hijab', 'schadenfreude', 'fjord'.

However, let's look again at 'house'. Are houses really so universal? Think of an English 'house' and you are likely to imagine a thatched cottage or a suburban terrace or semi. The cottage might be timber framed; the terrace or semi might be built of brick and roofed with slate. But a Greek σπίτι will probably look different: it might be covered in white render, with shutters on the windows, and a flat roof. Linguists have a technical term for these images that tend to pop up in response to words: 'prototypes'. Words that have the same propositional meaning can suggest different prototypes.

Propositional meaning and prototypes are just two aspects of the meanings of words. There are several others, and they can be given various labels. 'Expressive' or 'connotational' meaning names the feeling that attaches to a word. When I say 'that's my home' I mean something different from 'that's my house', even if I am pointing at the same building. Part of the difference is a matter of propositional meaning: a 'home' is likely to be a permanent or habitual dwelling place whereas a 'house' need not be. But the more important difference is expressive: 'house' is unemotive but 'home' suggests feelings of warmth and belonging.

Other languages don't handle this feeling in the same way. An Italian dictionary will tell you that *casa* is the word for 'house'. But at the end of an evening, when I might say 'I'm going home', an

Italian would still use *casa—torno a casa*. In this instance the *casa* is as likely to be a flat as a house: it is the feeling of home that is the dominant meaning. A stronger feeling, homesickness, is likely to come out in different words again. Imagine an English 10-year-old on a disastrous school trip—tired, hungry, weeping, he says, 'I just want to go home!' An Italian child in the same situation might possibly say she wants to go back *a casa* but it's more likely she'd wail something different: *voglio tornare dalla mamma!* ('I want to go back to mum!').

As even these everyday examples show, the relationship between words and meanings is very complex. 'Meaning' has many aspects. They can be distinguished with technical terms like the ones I have been using—propositional and expressive meaning and prototypes—but the relationship between those categories is complicated and the borders between them are blurred. Even within a language a word's meanings shift as it is used in different circumstances; when it is translated into another language more radically different meanings will appear. Arabic has distinctive means for talking about what we would call homes and houses. 'بيت' (*bayt*) tends to emphasize the fact of spending the night in a place, while 'دار' (*dar*) and 'منزل' (*manzil*) point to family and tribe, as well as dwelling. If I say that *dar* means 'house' I downplay all the actual differences in meaning between the two words. All I am really saying is that *dar* is a word you might use to translate 'house', and vice versa.

So translation does not translate the meanings of words; at least, not in the sense of taking the meaning of a word in one language and finding a word with the same meaning in another. Many words are like 'scone', with propositional meanings that can't be matched by any single words in other languages. So the translator performs some workaround, explaining the troublesome source-language word, or simply pulling it across into the language of the translation. More often, a reasonable overlap of propositional meaning can be achieved. But even when this is the case, the expressive meaning and prototypes are likely to differ. The translator can look at other words in the same 'lexical set'—that is words with related senses—in search of the best match for the whole bundle of meanings evoked by the source. In different circumstances, *casa* might best be translated as 'house' or 'flat' or 'apartment' or 'place' or 'home'. But even the best match will inevitably be different in some ways.

Often, the context helps readers to attach at least roughly the right sort of meaning to the word. In fact we make this sort of adjustment all the time without realizing it. If you are reading a book set in Algeria you can guess that the 'house' the protagonists are living in is not very likely to be half-timbered with a thatched roof and bay windows and wisteria growing over the door. The novelist Christine Brooke-Rose makes a joke about this aspect of translation in her multilingual novel *Between*. The English protagonist is helping a Vatican priest to find the best Italian translation for 'cottage' (they are in the midst of the arduous process of annulling her Roman Catholic marriage, and are using French as a common language):

> — Un cottage? Que voulez-vous dire, un cottage? [A cottage? What do you mean, a cottage?]
>
> — Hé bien, mon père, une toute petite maison, à la campagne. [Well, father, it's a little house, in the country]
>
> ...
>
> Un cottage. The pale fat priest-interpreter looks over his half-spectacles made for reading the sheafs of notes before him. Un piccolo chalet. Va bene così? Un piccolo chalet? [A little chalet. Does that work? A little chalet?]
>
> — Va bene. Un piccolo chalet in Wiltshire. [That works. A little chalet in Wiltshire].

There are lots of ways in which 'chalet' does not mean the same as 'cottage'. To an English-speaking mind, the idea of a chalet in Wiltshire is deeply bizarre. And 'chalet' is not even really an

Italian word. But all the priest needs is a means of saying 'small house in the country' that is comprehensible to Italian speakers. The readers of the document he is writing will just have to realize for themselves that this 'chalet', in this context, is an English sort of building, not a Swiss one.

Words in contexts

In our 'chalet' example, the meaning of the word is altered by the sentence it appears in. This happens everywhere, in every language. When we translate, what matters to us is not some notional meaning that a given word might have in itself, but rather the meaning that it has in the sentence in front of us. Here are some examples:

> I'll run away
> I run a company
> I'll run some tests
> I'm running for office
> My stockings have run
> The ad will run in the paper tomorrow
> I'm going to run some errands
> Let me run you a bath
> You're running a risk!

'Run' means something quite different in each of these sentences. Other languages are likely to need several different words to translate it (for instance French might use *s'enfouir, diriger, mener, se présenter, filer, être publié, faire, faire couler, courir*). Translators are hardly ever faced with words in isolation, but rather longer stretches of language: phrases, sentences, paragraphs, chapters, books. The best translation will be the word that works best in this larger context.

Despite all these variations, we still tend to say that the French for 'run' is *courir*, and, more generally, that *the word for* 'X' in one language *is* 'Y' in another. When we learn a language in school we typically memorize lists of English and foreign words side by side. Small bilingual dictionaries also offer one word as the equivalent of another. Both these factors contribute to our habit of saying that one word 'means' the other, for instance that *courir* means 'run'. This is a perfectly effective way of learning vocabulary, but it is important to see that it relies on a misleading shorthand. We are not being given the *meaning* of *courir*. Instead, we are learning a word that can be used to translate *courir* in many circumstances, but by no means all. Big dictionaries like the *Oxford English Dictionary*, and big online resources like WordReference.com, will give a more varied picture, with many examples of 'run' taking on different meanings in different sentences. But the reality of language use is more complex still. Words are always being used in new contexts where they take on new meanings and have to be translated in different ways.

Fifty years ago, the linguist J. C. Catford came up with what is still the most helpful way of understanding this truth about translation. When we translate, we don't transfer something called meaning out of one language and into another. Rather, we find words that are *'interchangeable in a given situation'*. Where an Italian would say *torno a casa* I would say 'I'm going home'.

This way of looking at translation helps us see how to handle all the grammatical divergences which, even more than differences between words, prevent languages from neatly lining up. In English, we have singular and plural. In ancient Greek (and several modern languages including Arabic and Inuit) there are grammatical forms for singular, plural, and dual. If an ancient Greek wrote that ἀδελφώ were fighting you would know it was two brothers; if the ending of the noun was changed to ἀδελφοί you would know it was more than two. It's possible to think that this distinction is simply untranslatable: if you put just 'brothers' you lose the nuance, whereas if you put 'two brothers' (or alternatively 'more than two brothers') you turn a subtlety into something cumbersome. Catford's argument gives us confidence in opting for whichever choice best suits the situation: 'two brothers' if the number seems important, just 'brothers' if it does not.

English is closer to French than it is to Greek, but here too grammar arranges the world in disparate ways. An English child thinking, 'When I'm big I'll be happy,' mixes present and future tenses; a French child with the same dream has to put it all in the future: 'Quand je serai grand je serai heureux' ('When I will be big I will be happy'). This is just one of many divergences in the chronicling of time. Another area of difference is the choice of phrases made with nouns or verbs. In English I'd say 'when I get back'; in French I'd probably turn the verb into a noun 'à mon retour' ('on my return'). Phrasing gives some of the clearest examples of the virtues of Catford's approach—especially those peculiar phrases called 'idioms' where the whole has developed a meaning that is very different from the combined meanings of the words that make it up. 'Break a leg' does not *mean* 'good luck'. Rather, in a given situation, it can be used as a substitute for 'good luck!' The Italian *in bocca al lupo!* (literally 'in the mouth of the wolf') can be substituted for 'good luck!' in the same way.

Idioms are extreme manifestations of the idiomatic quality that permeates every language. In English people tend to say 'strictly forbidden' rather than 'thoroughly forbidden' or 'completely forbidden' or 'severely forbidden'. There is no grammatical or semantic reason why it should be those two words that typically go together in this way. Other languages make different choices: the French would be *formellement interdit*; the German, *streng verboten*; the Italian, *severamente proibito*. If you had to translate these phrases back into English, what would you do? You could choose to follow the dictionary meanings of the separate words, that is use the English words that correspond to these individual foreign words in most contexts. This would give you 'formally

33

forbidden', 'stringently forbidden', and 'severely prohibited'. This sort of translation is what we usually call 'literal' and it can be useful in various ways—for instance if you want to draw attention to the differences between languages. Or you could follow the Catford line and go for 'strictly forbidden' because it is the phrase that is generally used in English in the same situation. This is the sort of translation that is usually called 'free' or 'idiomatic'.

How does the idea of 'meaning' fit into this translation decision? Is it better to say that *formellement interdit* means 'formally forbidden' or that it means 'strictly forbidden'? Well, let's remember that when we say 'means' here we are not really giving the meaning; all we are doing is providing English words that we hope other people will understand. If they don't, we can offer more words, perhaps in the form of an explanation; but we can't ever get at the 'meaning' itself. A better description would be to say that 'formally forbidden' translates the words *formellement interdit*, whereas 'strictly forbidden' translates the 'utterance' or 'speech act', that is what the French words are being used to do.

We use words all the time to do things that are quite different from what the dictionary tells us they mean. The context is crucial here. If I say 'Brilliant!' when I drop a cup of coffee on the book I am reading I don't mean anything like the dictionary definition of the word 'brilliant'. I am coming out with an utterance that means something much more like the dictionary definition of 'Damn!'

The words we use to end letters are another, more formalized example. When I write 'yours sincerely' I am not likely to be making any special claim to devotion or truthfulness: I am just using the standard formula that accomplishes the speech act of bringing a letter to an end, to be followed by a signature. The idiomatic French translation of this phrase in this situation has nothing to do with sincerity: it is likely to be *bien à vous* ('good to you'). An Italian would probably write *cordiali saluti* ('friendly salutations') while a

Chinese would put '此致 敬礼' (*ci-zi jing-li*—'thus concludes the above: I salute you').

The idea that translation supplies words that are '*interchangeable in a given situation*' helps us to see why these quite different phrases can count as translations of one another. Nevertheless, Catford's definition is not perfect. There is more than this to the question of what translation translates.

Purpose

Imagine that you have been employed as a translator by The Morris Ring, which is an association of traditional English Morris- and sword-dancing clubs. You are required to translate, into any language other than English, the following instructions about how to prepare to dance a 'jig':

> Pull up your socks (no wrinkles).
>
> Check your bell pads are secure (we all have had a loose set of bells around our ankle). If this happens, make light of it—you could try shaking your foot to dislodge the bell pad and announcing that you have made up a new dance. If this fails, indicate to your muso to stop playing (if he has not already done so because he cannot play for laughing), remove the bell pad and place it beside your hat. DO NOT throw it away. Ask your muso either to start again from the beginning, or from a suitable point before the incident. In this way your confidence will be restored.
>
> Check your hat is in good condition.
>
> Make sure that your shoes, hankies and tabard / baldrics are clean, if not, SWAP them.
>
> Leave your tankard behind.

Notice how much knowledge is taken for granted: what a 'jig' is; where the 'bell pads' are secured unless they work loose; who the 'muso' is'; where the 'hat' will have been placed; what the 'hankies' and 'tabard / baldrics' and 'tankard' are, exactly, and how they should be used.

Taken in isolation, each of these little conundrums is like the difficulty posed by 'scone', which we explored in the last section. The Morris-dancing terms each refer to a bit of 'realia', that is to an item which is specific to English culture—and a specialized strand of English culture at that. As we saw, it is often tricky to find good equivalents for such words in other languages. Translating them is likely to involve either explanation or adoption of the whole English word, or both.

However, if you take them all together, these Morris-dancing words pose another difficulty. They all belong to a distinct situation. In fact, they help to bring that situation into being: Morris dancing would not be what it is without these words to shape it. And this whole situation is unlikely to have close analogues in other cultures. It follows that readers of a translation will probably find the whole scenario difficult to imagine and understand. (English readers who are not Morris-dancing aficionados may well feel something of the same perplexity.)

This example reveals a problem with the idea that translation involves finding words that are 'interchangeable in a given situation'. What if the situation is not 'given'—that is if it is not readily understandable—and so itself needs to be translated? The situations envisaged by Catford tend to seem simple and easily reproducible. For instance, he explains that the Burushaki language of North West Pakistan does not have words meaning 'brother' and 'sister'. Instead, Burushaki speakers say *a-cho* for a sibling of the same sex as the speaker and *a-yas* for a sibling of the opposite sex from the speaker. Catford points out that, although 'brother' and *a-yas* cannot be said to mean the same, they can still be interchangeable in a given situation, for instance when someone is introducing her relatives. This sort of situation seems pretty straightforward. It is easy to imagine yourself stepping into it and making the introductions in your own words.

But the Morris-dancing situation is different. How could a notional Japanese or Turkish translator set about finding words used in that same situation in Japan or Turkey? The situation itself needs to be translated. There are various ways of doing this. The translator might look for a situation which, although necessarily different in many respects, has at least some elements in common with Morris dancing—perhaps Japanese Odori or Turkish Halay dances. The preparations for the jig might then be re-imagined, with 'tabard', 'bell-pads', and the rest being replaced by accessories appropriate to the new context. This sort of cultural transposition is not unusual in the translation of children's books.

However, this is unlikely to be what the Morris Ring, if they commissioned a translation, would have in mind. They are likely to think that the information about their particular kind of dance is of crucial importance. How the translator meets this concern will depend on the intended audience. If the translation is aimed at people who are somehow knowledgeable about Morris dancing even though they don't speak English, then the translator might confine himself to translating the words on the page, leaving the technical terms unchanged. But if the aim is to reach out to a new audience who don't know about Morris dancing then more will need to be done. The 'bell-pads', etc., will need to be made comprehensible through explanation and perhaps photographs. Some description of Morris dancing in general will need to be added, either woven into the main text or given as notes.

So the 'situation' (or context) of the words that are being translated is not the only thing that determines how translation should be done. The purpose of the translation is crucial too (sometimes 'purpose' is called *skopos* because this line of thought was developed by a German theorist, Hans Vermeer). Translations vary enormously according to their purpose, and most of us are so used to this that we don't even notice it.

Purpose in subtitling, theatre, and advertising

The purpose of subtitles in films and TV programmes is to allow viewers to follow the dialogue. Often a character will speak too fast for every single word to be translated in subtitles, especially as they have to harmonize with the visuals, changing when the shot changes, and never obscuring too much of the frame. In a scene from the French police drama *Engrenages*, translated as *Spiral*, the fast-talking Capitaine Laure Berthaud says: 'Il ne nous manque que l'adresse dans le seizième où le taxi l'a prise—c'est une question d'heures.' ('We are only missing the address in the sixteenth arrondissement where the taxi picked her up—it's a matter of hours.') The subtitle reads: 'We'll soon have the address where the cab picked her up.' Viewers implicitly recognize the constraints that subtitles are under and the purpose for which they are designed. We take it for granted that they cannot always render every spoken word.

Purpose is what mainly determines whether a translation is more literal or more free (to use the familiar loose words); more of a 'metaphrase' or more of a 'paraphrase' (to borrow those terms of Dryden's which I discussed in the last chapter). And purpose influences what particular kind of freedom or closeness a translation pursues. The dominant purpose of a translation for the theatre is to work in performance, so this sort of translation typically aims for dramatic effect. Tony Harrison's version of Aeschylus' *Agamemnon*, performed at the National Theatre in London in 1981, has a vocal, rhythmic pulse which gets going as soon as the watchman speaks at the start of the play:

> No end to it all, though all year I've muttered
> my pleas to the gods for a long groped for end.

> Wish it were over, this waiting, this watching,
> twelve weary months, night in and night out,
> crouching and peering, head down like a bloodhound,
> paws propping muzzle, up here on the palace…

By contrast, Alan H. Sommerstein's translation was done for the Loeb library of parallel text classics, and is designed primarily as a help towards reading the Greek:

> I beg the gods to give me release from this misery—from my long year of watch-keeping, during which I've spent my nights on the Atreidae's roof, resting on my elbows like a dog, and come to know thoroughly the throng of stars of the night…

Back in 1877, the poet Robert Browning published a translation with a different purpose again. He wanted to make his readers see what a strange, difficult writer Aeschylus was, and what a gap separated ancient Greek culture from Victorian England:

> The gods I ask deliverance from these labours,
> Watch of a year's length whereby, slumbering through it
> On the Atreidai's roofs on elbow,—dog-like—
> I know of nightly star-groups the assemblage.

These translations of the same source text are very divergent from one another. The reason is the difference in their purposes.

Advertisements typically have a very clear purpose: to sell. And so purpose has an especially dominant role in their translation. In 2011, the drinks company Innocent launched its new, branded orange juice with adverts like the one in Figure 2.

Key elements are the brand-name 'Innocent', the halo logo, the shape of the bottle, the orange made to look like a face with the cut segment as a smile, and the vibe of good humour and mild sexiness which the advert connects to the brand via the puns on

2. An Innocent drinks advert: 'Innocent's new squeeze'.

le jus innocent pressé avec amour

3. An Innocent drinks advert in French: 'Pressé avec amour'.

'juicy' (which can mean 'erotic' or 'naughty') and 'squeeze' (which means boyfriend or girlfriend as well as the squeezing of oranges that has produced the drink).

A couple of years later, the same product was launched in France, and the publicity campaign needed translating. The bottle, the logo, and the image could all be reproduced exactly, as could the brand-name, for 'innocent' is a French word as well as an English one. But what of the all-important puns? 'Squeeze' and 'juicy' wouldn't have the same charge if translated literally, so the French campaign took a different tack, as we can see in Figure 3.

Pressé avec amour ('squeezed with love') has a mild frisson; but it is the little footnote that makes a pun. *Jus-ré* suggests *juré*, best translated as 'I promise' or 'I swear'—the sort of thing that kids

41

4. Another Innocent drinks advert in French: 'Paris jus t'aime'.

might say in a playground. The play on *jus* continues in other adverts from the same campaign such as the one shown in Figure 4.

Here, *jus t'aime* is almost the same as *je t'aime* (I love you). The words are quite different from the English advert. But the mood, and the purpose behind it, have been very successfully translated.

Chapter 4
Forms, identities, and interpretations

Icons

Neither the picture on the front of an Innocent fruit juice bottle
nor the bottle itself need translating (see Figures 2, 3, and 4). They
can simply be transported from England to France. And yet they
both have significance. The bottle looks different from an average
bottle of juice, which suggests that this is a distinctive product
from a prestige brand. With its flaring neck, it resembles a carafe
of wine and so has connotations of adulthood and good taste. The
picture of the orange with the cut segment is recognizably a
face, with two dots for eyes and a halo coloured green to signify
an environmental sort of innocence. The image looks like a text
message smiley, and making a face out of an orange is rather
a childish thing to do: these youthful connotations mingle
humorously with the sophisticated shape of the bottle, helping the
product to appeal to a wide variety of consumers.

All these suggestions are as recognizable in France as in England.
But this is not because shapes and images are understandable
everywhere without translation. Rather, it is because French and
English cultures have so much in common: wine, other fruit
juices, mobile phones, environmentalism, images of childhood,
and the tradition of Christian iconography that produced the halo.
If the bottle were transported to a Muslim, Arabic-speaking

country such as Saudi Arabia, where Christian symbolism is alien and wine drinking largely illegal then it might be necessary to translate, not only the words, but the picture and even the shape of the bottle.

In the technical idiom of semiotics, the meaning of pictures and shapes is said to be 'iconic' rather than 'conventional'. A picture of a mountain looks like a mountain, whereas the word 'mountain' means 'mountain' because speakers of English agree to use that combination of sounds and letters for that purpose.

Yet the distinction between 'iconic' and 'conventional' is not absolute. Some learning and agreement are necessary to understand icons. Red means danger because it is the colour of fire, but fire has other colours too: orange, yellow, and any number of shades in between. It is social convention that has selected red and attached this particular significance to it. And it is social convention that has limited the situations in which red means danger to signs and related contexts. We don't think that someone wearing a red T-shirt must be dangerous. There is a similar mixture of iconic and conventional in the Innocent drink bottle. It looks like a carafe, and the circle above the orange looks like a halo. But it is culture that has made those shapes suggest wine and saintliness.

Still, images are usually more widely understandable than words. And so sign systems that combine iconic and conventional meanings can become simple, international languages. The International Organization for Standardization (ISO), based in Geneva, creates signs for use across 164 countries: you are likely to see them in airports and tourist destinations. Figure 5 reveals a graduation from more iconic to more conventional kinds of meaning.

The 'no diving' sign is very iconic: to understand it you only need to know what diving looks like and to be able to read its simple visual

44

5. International Graphic Symbols.

style. The picture in the 'emergency exit' sign is less specific and so
needs interpreting in relation to its context. If it were placed on the
outside of a bomb shelter it might mean 'way in': it is international
agreement that restricts its use to the insides of buildings and so
allows people to learn its intended meaning. The 'information' sign
is more conventional still. ISO must have failed to come up with a
suitable image for giving information and so chose the first letter of
the relevant word in English and a few other languages. Speakers of
different languages have to translate and learn this sign just as they
would the whole word 'information'.

The written forms of some languages, like Egyptian hieroglyphics
and Chinese script, include markedly iconic elements. One
such script was used by the Algonkin, Iroquoian, and Sioux nations
of North America. Speed was represented by a spiral, war by a
diagonal cross, prosperity by a vertical line with three cross-bars,
and so on. Figure 6 shows an extract from a text known as the
Walum Olum (*Red Score*) of the Lenape-Algonkin, a list of chiefs
(*sachems*) and their exploits apparently made during the 16th and
17th centuries (there are debates about its authenticity). In the
translation, Gordon Brotherston has echoed the shapes of the
pictograms in the structure of his English: each symbol gets a line,
and each line is divided in two.

The fact that English can take on at least a trace of the forms of
picture-writing shows us that verbal languages have iconic

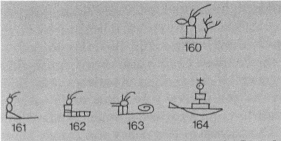

160

161   162   163   164

Great Beaver was sachem, remaining in Sassafras land

White-Body was sachem, at the Shore
Friend-to-all was sachem, he did good
He-Makes-Mistakes was sachem, he arrived with speed
At this time whites came on the eastern sea

6. An Algonkin account of whites entering northern America, 17th century. Transcribed by Gordon Brotherston and translated by Brotherston in collaboration with Ed Dorn.

elements too. In Chinese and related languages, the topic of a sentence is typically placed at the beginning:

那棵	樹	葉子	大,	所以	我	不	喜歡
Nàkē	shù	yèzi	dà,	suǒyǐ	wǒ	bù	xǐhuān

That tree [the] leaves [are] big so I don't like

In English, physical proximity determines which adjectives or adverbs belong with which nouns or verbs. 'I swim in the still lake' means something quite different from 'I still swim in the lake'. In Latin, by contrast, words can be arranged in more varied ways because they are connected by their endings. Take Virgil's line:

maioresque cadunt altis de montibus umbrae

[greater and fall high from mountains shadows]

(*Eclogues* I, 84)

Maiores ('greater') belongs with *umbrae* ('shadows') and *altis* ('high') with *montibus* ('mountains'). An idiomatic English translation—for instance 'and longer shadows are cast by high mountains'—would have to alter the expressive patterning of the words.

Comics and verse form

We use words to form patterns and shapes all the time. Newspaper headlines grab our attention because they are printed big and bold. Websites use colour and animation to guide our eyes around the screen. Even this little book that you are holding structures your reading with chapter headings, subheadings, and paragraphs. These organizational elements of language are usually not very hard to translate, though they do vary from culture to culture just like the shapes of bottles. Script reads in different directions in different writing systems: Arabic starts at the top right and goes from right to left; Chinese starts at the top right and goes from top to bottom; Roman script starts at the top left and goes from left to right. The way a text is arranged alters with translation between these modes of writing. There are differences between languages that share the same script too: for instance, translations from English to French usually have to shift the contents page from the front of a book to the back.

In comics and graphic novels, the interrelation between writing and iconic patterning is more intricate. Figure 7 shows a series of frames from David Lewis and Toren Smith's English translation of Hayao Miyazaki's *Nausicaä and the Valley of the Wind*: the Japanese page layout is unchanged, so we have to read from right to left. The heroine, Nausicaä, is hearing voices, as well as coming out with thoughts and words of her own: the different shapes of the speech bubbles prompt us to distinguish between these various sorts of language, and to intuit the feelings that attach to them.

The octagonal speech bubble in the first frame implies that Nausicaä is trying to get a grip on what is happening to her, imposing a

7. *Nausicaä and the Valley of the Wind*, drawn by Hayao Miyazaki, translated by David Lewis and Toren Smith.

geometrical level of order on her sensations. In the next frame, ordinary thoughts are expressed in a standard bubble; but in the frame that follows the paint-splash-shaped bubbles suggest anxious shouts. In the fourth frame, Nausicaä reverts to an ordinary speech bubble, shifting from shock to sympathy in a move that is typical of her character.

Meanwhile, the jagged and fuzzy bubbles of the disembodied voices suggest their distorted, hallucinatory mode of being: in the fourth frame, the sound seems to turn into a sort of light—perhaps an *ignis fatuus* or firefly—between Nausicaä's hands. In the two frames that follow, Japanese characters have been left untranslated because they form part of the image: a key explains that the sound represented in the first is *kiiiin*, translated as 'vweeeen', and in the second *kyululululu*, translated as 'bwatatata'. Still, the English-speaking reader can get the point that some sort of embodied noise, or perhaps just something making a noise, is whizzing past Nausicaä: she can't see what it is, but she feels that something is there, almost as though written characters, little bundles of sound, are flying through the air around her.

The series of frames shows the continuity between shapes that are used to make pictures and shapes that are part of verbal language. This is especially clear in the second-last frame, where an exclamation that can be translated, 'AA!', blends into punctuation marks that are shared between English and Japanese, '!!', which then connect to Japanese characters that have been stretched so as to form a picture of aggressive motion, and have been left untranslated because they are part of the visual composition. Visual cues also matter within the speech bubbles. We realize that words in bold type (as in the second frame) are more emphatic than words printed normally; we feel that an exclamation mark with a line to itself ('killed / us / !') is slightly different from one that is attached to the end of a word ('he / killed / us!').

There is also significance in the way the speech bubbles are arranged. When Nausicaä speaks in jagged bubbles in the fourth frame it is as though the energy of the similarly jagged bubbles in the first frame is coming out through her voice. And the series of fuzzy bubbles in the second frame creates a pattern that envelopes her face and her thoughts: it is a sequence of visual rhyme.

These visual patterns can be left untranslated because they rely on conventions of understanding that are shared between English and Japanese. Post-war Japanese manga are influenced by American and English comics, and vice versa: they have a common visual language.

In poetry, form works in a surprisingly similar way. The sonnet and other verse forms circulated among European languages from the medieval period onwards: they became a repertoire that was largely held in common. Just as with the *Nausicaä* cartoon, form in poetry enables words and syntax to collaborate with visual and aural patterns to produce complex meanings.

For this reason, translators of poetry sometimes choose to keep the rhyme scheme, in the same way as the translation of *Nausicaä* preserves the visual patterning. But this isn't an obvious decision. If you reproduce rhyme you are likely to have to sacrifice other important elements of your source text. And languages have differing propensities for rhyme, so the same poetic form can feel quite different in different tongues.

English translations of Dante are a good example. The *Divine Comedy* is written in a complicated rhyme scheme called *terza rima*. The rhymes go ABABCBCDCD, and so on, and on—as you can see in the first six lines (translations follow a bit further down):

Translation

Nel mezzo del cammin di nostra vita	A
mi ritrovai per una selva oscura,	B
ché la diritta via era smarrita.	A
Ahi quanto a dir qual era è cosa dura	B
esta selva selvaggia e aspra e forte	C
che nel pensier rinova la paura!	B

Vita rhymes with *smarrita*. *Oscura* rhymes with *dura* and *paura*. *Forte* starts a new triplet of rhyme which continues after the end of this quotation.

One option for a translator is to recreate this rhyme scheme in English. It's a challenge, but many have risen to it, including the crime novelist Dorothy L. Sayers in her *Hell* of 1949:

> Midway this way of life we're bound upon,
> I woke to find myself in a dark wood,

> Where the right road was wholly lost and gone.
> Ay me! how hard to speak of it—that rude
>> And rough and stubborn forest! the mere breath
>> Of memory stirs the old fear in the blood;

The chain reaction of the rhyme certainly gets going in these lines, but other aspects of the poetry have had to shift to enable this to happen. Dante doesn't say that he is 'bound upon' the way or path of life—just that he is in the middle of it: Sayers needs 'upon' for the rhyme. It's the same with 'wholly lost and gone', standing in for just one word, *smarrita*, which corresponds to 'lost'. Dante says nothing about 'breath' or about 'blood': these words too are there for the rhyme, and they bring new images with them. That's not all. Keeping the same rhyme scheme doesn't mean that the verse feels the same. Dante's rhymes are soft because, like most Italian words, they end on an unaccented syllable (this used to be called 'feminine' rhyme; the modern technical term is 'paroxytonic'). And rhymes are easier to find in Italian than in English. So *terza rima* feels more intrusive in Sayers's English than in Dante's Italian: it is a performance rather than a pulse.

A century earlier, the American poet Henry Wadsworth Longfellow chose a different verse form for his Dante translation:

> Midway upon the journey of our life
>> I found myself within a forest dark,
>> For the straightforward pathway had been lost.
> Ah me! how hard a thing it is to say
>> What was this forest savage, rough, and stern,
>> Which in the very thought renews the fear.

Since Longfellow doesn't have to juggle rhymes he can make his words and syntax correspond more closely to Dante's. On the other hand, the forward impetus of *terza rima* has been lost. The challenge of poetic form gives us a stark instance of a familiar truth: translation never provides an exact reproduction of any element of the source text. It is always a matter of shifts and alterations: a metamorphosis, not a copy. Not even a rhyme scheme can be recreated without some difference seeping in.

And not sentences either, since they have form too. I discovered this to my cost in one of my own early ventures in translation. When I was a graduate student, I was commissioned to revise a translation of Alessandro Manzoni's great 19th-century novel *I promessi sposi* (*The Betrothed*) that had been done by Archibald Colquhoun back in 1951. Manzoni is a master of the long, winding sentence, and I wanted to try to reproduce this movement for English readers. I started out by making the structure of the English sentences match the Italian as closely as possible, semi-colon for semi-colon, full stop for full stop. Then I sat back to read what I had created. It was horrible!—the feeling was quite different. Where the Italian cascaded, the English congealed. I realized that I could give a better impression of the flow of Manzoni's writing by handling the syntax slightly differently. The movement of prose is not only a matter of sentence structure, just as the feel of poetry involves more than metre and rhyme.

Identity

Longfellow and Dorothy L. Sayers chose different aspects of Dante's identity as a writer to represent in English. Readers of Sayers's translation encounter a virtuoso of the *terza rima* form; readers of Longfellow's find a devotee of a plain and lapidary style. We might ask: which is the more true to Dante? Which is the more Dantesque? The answer is that they are both equally true. Dante's identity as a writer is complex: the two translations reveal different sides of it.

This simple observation is a challenge to how we think about identity in translation. Discussions of the topic have almost always made it seem that the source text has a given, unitary identity, and that translations can be calibrated as either being faithful to it or departing from it. Whatever analytical terms are used to describe the issue, the either/or construction persists. Either a translation is close or it is free. As the German philosopher Friedrich Schleiermacher put it in 1813: either (*entweder*) it moves the reader towards the writer (*bewegt den Leser ihm entgegen*), or (*oder*) it moves the writer towards the reader (*bewegt den Schriftsteller ihm entgegen*). Either it is 'foreignizing'—to use the contemporary terminology of translation studies—or it is 'domesticating'.

However, both the Sayers and the Longfellow translations bridge these binaries. Sayers is 'close' and 'foreignizing' and 'moves the reader towards Dante' because she uses *terza rima*; she is 'free' and 'domesticating' and 'moves Dante towards the reader' in her choice of words. Longfellow is 'close', 'foreignizing', etc., because he writes with a plainness unusual in English-language poetry at that time; he is 'free', 'domesticating', etc., because he eschews *terza rima* for blank verse. In general terms, the same is true of all translations: every translation is a mixture of foreignization and domestication.

There are two basic reasons why this is so. The first is that every translation mediates between the source text and the receiving language and culture. The translation cannot completely reproduce the source text in all its distinctiveness and foreignness: that would mean not translating it at all. And the translation can't completely domesticate the source text either: it can't abolish its distinctiveness and foreignness completely. To do that would be to write a new, different text. So all translations operate in conditions of between-ness: they all inhabit a middle ground.

The second reason is that both the source text and the receiving language—that is the entities on either side of this no-man's land of translation—are complex and hard to define. There isn't one pole called 'foreign' and another pole called 'domestic', with a single line that can be drawn between them. The degree of 'foreignization' or 'domestication' cannot be measured on a single scale.

Think of how many ways there are of using English (or any language): dialects from Yorkshire to multicultural London English, degrees of formality from a courtroom to the pub, registers from medical language to racing punditry, idioms that vary from person to person, the multitude of literary genres and writing styles. To say that a text is being 'domesticated', that is translated into unchallenging, familiar English, is to beg the questions: What sort of English? Familiar to whom?

And think of how many ways there are of producing a source text, whether it is a spoken utterance or a piece of writing. I might use any of the kinds of language just mentioned: the 'me' I am inhabiting and presenting to the world—that is my identity—will vary accordingly. I might, like roughly half the people in the world, habitually use two or more languages, switching between them according to context, topic, or whim. In this case, the role of language in constructing rather than simply conveying identity is obvious.

The identity I build through language and other aspects of my behaviour also depends on how my words and actions are received by listeners, readers, and social institutions. A joke that some find funny will seem to others lame. An explanation can seem helpful to some people, patronizing to others, and incomprehensible to others again. As for writing, it is vulnerable to being taken in all sorts of different ways: one reader's cliché seems a touch of brilliance to another; one's greatness is another's tedium. An article that I have written, and that I think to be pretty good, might be spiked by the magazine that commissioned it. An application for a new job might succeed or fail. All these reactions are among the processes by which identity takes on definition in a given context (or is 'performed', to use the word preferred by critical theory). They are part of what you can say about what a piece of writing or a person is.

This means that a translator is never faced with a given identity to translate. The acts of reading and interpreting and judging and rewording that make up translation all play a part in defining the identity that the translation will represent (Sayers defines Dante as a poet of *terza rima*; Longfellow defines him as a poet of plain style). Inevitably, the translator will draw out some aspects more than others. Some aspects will provoke the effort of doing something new in the receiving language, of adopting a 'foreignizing' tactic; others will be skipped or left in softer focus. As this happens, the translator builds a style in the receiving language which will have its own mix of distinctiveness and conventionality. And it will inevitably seem more 'domesticated' or more 'foreignized' to some readers or listeners than to others.

The translation's context and purpose have a decisive influence on these processes. Asylum interviews are intensely focused on establishing some aspects of the identity of the interviewees—but only some. It matters where the asylum-seekers are from and whether they have been subjected to violence or the threat of it. Other aspects of their identity might matter too: dialect, sexuality, ethnicity, family grouping. But probably not their individual styles of speech or writing, or their particular skills and tastes. The guidelines for interpreters in the Finnish immigration service make the institutional context clear:

> The asylum seeker's matter must be interpreted into another language comprehensively and accurately, so that the authority can reach a fair decision in the matter of a person seeking international protection. Therefore the interpreter is in a key position, communicating messages in situations which have a bearing on the rest of the asylum seeker's life. The interpreter's task is to faithfully and accurately interpret the message from one language to another.

What is needed is the presentation of 'matter' or 'message', rather than style or idiom. And what counts as 'matter' or 'message' are facts that can be used to determine an asylum claim.

With an ethnographic study, the purpose and the aspects of identity that come to the fore are completely different. During the 1870s, in South Africa, Wilhelm Bleek and Lucy Lloyd conducted interviews with several members of the Bushman people: |A!kungta, ||Kabbo, |Hang#kass'o, Dia!kwain, !Kweiten ta, and |Xaken-ang. Bleek and Lloyd wanted, first, to learn the !Xam language spoken by the Bushman people, then to begin to understand their culture and write down their traditional stories. The over-arching context for this endeavour was violent: southern Africa was subject to British and Boer imperialism, and Bleek and Lloyd were only able to encounter their interlocutors because they had been arrested. Still, insofar as it was possible within this brutal environment, the interviews seem to have been conducted courteously and attentively. The Bushman narrators lived in Bleek and Lloyd's house—albeit under guard—and the discussions with each took place over several months.

The Bushman people and the ethnographers had only a smattering of Afrikaans in common. They communicated at first by pointing to objects and to pictures, until Bleek and Lloyd could transcribe the Bushman words and learn them. Transcription required the invention of new characters to record the clicks and gutturals characteristic of !Xam: in the names I have just given, '|' indicates a dental click, '!' a cerebral click (i.e. one made by the tongue against the roof of the palate), and '#' a palatal click, i.e. one made by the tip of the tongue against the termination of the palate at the gums. The transcription of the stories, published in 1911 as *Specimens of Bushman Folklore*, uses all these signs and more, and they appear also among the English words of the parallel text translation. Here is the start of '!Kó-g!nuin-tára, Wife of the Dawn's Heart Star, Jupiter', narrated by ||Kabbo and translated by Lloyd.

> They sought for *!hāken*,* they were digging out *!hāken*. They went about, sifting *!hāken*, while they were digging out *!hāken*. And, when the larvae of the *!hāken* ( ) were intending to go in (to the

earth which was underneath the little hillock), they collected together, they sifted the larvae of the *!hāken* on the hunting ground.

*!hāken resembles "rice" (ie "Bushman rice"); its larvae are like (those of) "Bushman rice". *!hāken* is a thing to eat; there is nothing as nice as it is, when it is fresh.

The translation gives English readers a new word for a foodstuff they do not know and cannot name ('Bushman rice' is live ant larvae). And it gives us a sense of the reiterative modes of *!Xam* storytelling—or at least storytelling as it was done at that time, in that genre, by *||Kabbo*.

These are details that an asylum interview is likely to ignore. But we can't say that the ethnographic text is a truer translation of the speaker's identity. Rather, it draws out different aspects according to different conventions for different purposes. Of course, it needs to be attentive, and it needs not to make mistakes. The same is true of interpreting in an asylum interview: both modes of translation can be done more or less well. But translating more or less well isn't a matter of taking an identity that is given and fixed, and reproducing it with a greater or lesser degree of accuracy. Instead, translation joins in a performance of identity, which is always situated and relational, and extends it into a different context, time, and language.

An interpretation

Reviews of translated books usually don't expend more than a cursory word on the translation itself—but when they do, they often find something to object to. One striking instance was the *Times Literary Supplement* (*TLS*)'s review of Jamie McKendrick's 2007 translation of Giorgio Bassani's 1962 novel *Il giardino dei Finzi-Contini* (*The Garden of the Finzi-Contini*). The novel explores friendship and love between Jewish teenagers in Ferrara in the 1930s; the reviewer, Dan Gunn, doesn't like the words that McKendrick gives these characters to speak. Gunn finds it impossible to imagine that members of a cultured family such as the Finzi-Contini would use phrases like 'he looked like a right little wimp', 'utter bullshit', or 'no way!'; and he finds it not 'even remotely conceivable' that a well-read character like Micòl would say to the narrator 'you make off to make out, round at your true love's'. The issue here isn't a mistake about the meanings of the words, but something more subtle: a matter of tone.

Let's look more closely at the last quotation, with the Italian alongside McKendrick's translation. The narrator, by now at university in Bologna, is chatting to Micòl, the richer and more sophisticated girl whom he loves but who feels only friendliness towards him:

Translation

> Io, per esempio, appena posso prendo il treno e filo a Bologna...
>
> [As for me, whenever I can, I take the train and make off to Bologna...]

And she replies:

> Filerai a *filare*, va' là, confessa: dalla morosa'
>
> [Go on, tell the truth, you make off to *make out*, round at your true love's]

All the tension of their relationship sparks in her cruelly jokey interruption, with its wordplay between *filerai* in the sense of 'you will go or head off to' and *filare* in the sense of 'go out with, flirt with, get together with', and with its wry choice of the decorous word *morosa* ('beloved' or 'true love').

As it seems to me, McKendrick continues this performance of identity into English very successfully—certainly more so than the earlier translation by William Weaver which gives plain equivalents

of the propositional meaning but drops the expressive energy of
the exchange:

> You slip off to see your girl friend, go on. Confess.

But that is not how it seems to the *TLS* reviewer. The McKendrick
translation that strikes me as brilliantly suggesting what is going
on in this exchange strikes him as inappropriately slangy.

I don't want to quibble about which opinion is right—or more
right. The important thing to see is the degree to which each view
emerges from an interpretation. The way these characters speak
isn't simply there in Bassani's writing so that the translation can
be compared to it, and judged right or wrong. The connotations
of their speech have to be imagined by us as we read, paying
attention to the context and how the characters are behaving. Of
course, I feel that my interpretation is more in tune with the novel
than Dan Gunn's; but I recognize that it is an interpretation—that
the writing is open to being heard and understood differently.
My sense of 'the original' arises from a process of interpretation
and translation—and the same is true of everyone else's.

Reviewers of translations rarely keep this fact in mind. Typically, a
translation is either ticked off or praised (but usually ticked off)
for catching or failing to catch the 'tone' or 'spirit' of 'the original'.
But the original has no tone or spirit in itself: it takes readers to
imagine those qualities into being. In fact, there is fundamentally
no such thing as 'an original': there is only the source text that
gives rise to interpretations in collaboration with readers. So what
is really happening when a reviewer feels that a translation 'fails to
catch the tone of the original' is that the printed translation is
doing something different from the implicit translation that is in
the reviewer's mind.

As long as it is not the result of plain error, this variety ought
to be relished. If you know a book, why should you want a

translation to confirm the way you have already read it? Translations can show you, in amazing detail, how a text appears to other readers—interpretations that, like the *TLS* reviewer, you might not otherwise have been able to imagine. Translations can open up the nuances of meaning that the source text holds enclosed. They can enable the bud of it to bloom.

Here we come up against a cliché. 'Every translation is an interpretation' is almost as gaily bandied about as 'all communication is translation'. Just like that other received idea (which I discussed in Chapter 2), 'every translation is an interpretation' is only partly true. Interpretation and translation are intertwined, but they can also be distinguished.

The main idea of an 'interpretation' is that it opens out the meaning of the source text. This usually involves a change of genre or medium: an interpretation of a poem is usually a scholarly article or a school essay; an interpretation of a piece of music is usually a performance.

However, a translation of a novel is still a novel. To say 'every translation is an interpretation' is to downplay the fact that a translation is a text that needs to be interpreted in its turn. Of course, all texts need to be interpreted. A critical essay needs to be interpreted by its readers; a performance of a piece of music needs to be interpreted by its listeners. But there is a question of degree. Literary texts are open to a great variety of interpretations: that is part of what it means for them to be 'literary'. Critical essays give their readers fewer interpretive options. One reason for this is the way they are written: they don't, on the whole, play with ambiguity, fictionality, and form in the way that literary texts tend to. Another reason is that we all know how we are meant to read them: we read a critical essay in order to be given a view of the poem or book or artwork that it is about.

These invisible, implicit instructions bear on all language, both spoken and written. Different sorts of language-use ask to be handled in different ways. When a soldier hears a command from an officer, he knows he is meant to obey it. When we open a newspaper, we generally look for news. The invisible instruction manual for literary texts is longer, more scattered and self-contradictory than for other kinds of language. We know that we can do all sorts of things with poems, plays, and novels: read for the plot, be moved, be amused, be instructed, judge them, pay attention to their form, and so on, and on. This is why the interpretation of literary texts is always so vexed. And this is also why the translation of literary texts is so complicated and thought-provoking.

On the other hand, the use of speech in political negotiations is typically more focused on the transmission of meaning. This is how 'interpreting', in the sense of 'oral translation' connects to 'interpretation', in the sense of opening out the meaning of a written text. If the sort of speech that interpreters interpret is devoted to conveying meaning then a form of translation—interpreting—that gets the meaning clear will be appropriate. But in a literary text lots of things are going on other than the communication of meaning. With this sort of language use, translation and interpretation push in different directions. Translation is a mode of writing that tries to continue as much as possible of the source text's performance into another language. Interpretation focuses on opening out the meaning of the source text. An interpretation of a literary text is not likely to need much more interpretation in its turn. But a literary translation might well give rise to all sorts of interpretations.

These complicated interconnections between translation, interpretation, and ways of reading are especially visible in the practices of multilingual international organizations. The European Union conducts its business in all the official languages of its member states: the latest 'Consolidated Version' of its founding treaties exists in Bulgarian, Czech, Danish, Dutch, English, Estonian, Finnish, French, German, Greek, Hungarian, Irish, Italian, Latvian, Lithuanian, Maltese, Polish, Portuguese,

Romanian, Slovak, Slovenian, Spanish, and Swedish, with 'the texts in each of these languages being equally authentic'. The parallel texts are arrived at via a complex processes of translation, comparison, and negotiation. Each one is neither exactly an original nor exactly a translation, and they are all as close to one another as possible. But close is not identical. Where there are different languages there will necessarily be different meanings too.

Take even the most basic resolution, expressed in the preamble. Here is the English:

> RESOLVED to continue the process of creating an ever closer union among the peoples of Europe...

And here is the equally authentic French version:

> RÉSOLUS à poursuivre le processus créant une union sans cesse plus étroite entre les peuples de l'Europe...

Translation

But is 'an ever closer union' the same thing as 'une union sans cesse plus étroite'? It is hard to think of a better set of parallels: 'plus étroite' is the obvious translation of 'closer' in this context, and vice versa. Even so, the words push in slightly different directions. 'Étroit' has meanings that English uses different words to name: 'narrow' and 'tight'. 'Close' has stronger connotations of nearness and emotional intimacy than 'étroit': if you wanted to say that you feel close to someone in French you would probably use the word 'proche' instead. So if each of these texts were given to a different person to interpret it is likely that two slightly divergent visions of Europe would emerge. One might emphasize emotional union, the other, more closely interconnected institutions.

But, of course, that is not how these parallel texts in different languages are in fact used. Instead, they are all interpreted together. The European Parliament and its associated organizations jointly form an enormous 'interpretive community' whose job is to determine what 'an ever closer union', 'une union sans cesse plus étroite', and the cognate phrases in the other languages should all mean in terms of the political and legal measures that the European Union can carry out. So the fact that all these treaties are inter-translatable is not enough for them to have the same meaning. They need to be anchored in the same structures of interpretation as well.

Translation is not the same as interpretation. It is not the case that 'every translation is an interpretation'. But translation and interpretation are tightly intertwined. Translations incorporate interpretations—and provoke them. And where there are interpretations there is power, as we will see.

Chapter 5
Power, religion, and choice

Empires of interpretation

In 191 BCE, Phaeneas, an ambassador of the Aetolian people of western Greece, made a bad translation mistake. The Aetolians had lost a battle with the Romans, and Phaeneas was suing for peace. He told the Roman consul that the Aetolians gave themselves up to the 'trust' (*fides*) of the Roman people. As the Greek historian Polybius explains, Pheaneas didn't know what he was saying. He thought the Latin *fides* meant the same as its Greek cognate 'πίστις' (*pistis*), and that being in a relationship of *fides* with the Romans would entail some compromise, some mutually respectful negotiation. Not a bit of it. To the Romans, giving yourself over to *fides* meant unconditional surrender. Phaeneas was told to hand over two of his countrymen, and threatened with being put in chains.

When Phaeneas protested, the consul gave an interesting reply. He said that he wasn't in fact much bothered ('nec hercule... magnopere nunc curo') by the Greek understanding of the words *fides* and *pistis*. What mattered was that the Greeks had lost the battle, and he was in charge. When Phaeneas put the matter to a council of the Aetolians they felt there was no choice but to agree. The conqueror had to be obeyed.

This incident seems a long way from the negotiations in the European Union that I mentioned at the end of Chapter 4. With them, differences between versions of treaties in different languages are smoothed over by the enormous conversational apparatus of the European political project: there is one interpretive community that involves a wide range of people. Here, in the Phaeneas incident, there are separate communities, Greek and Roman; and they are not only different from one another but hostile. In the European Union, we had negotiation; here, we have war.

But in fact the two cases illustrate the same underlying principle. The choice of this or that word matters less than the power to determine meaning. If Phaeneas had got his translation right it would have made little, if any, difference: the Romans would still have been able to ignore or twist his speech and do what they wanted with the Aetolians. As Humpty Dumpty said, when it comes to meanings, all that matters is who is 'to be master'. Political empires are always also empires of interpretation.

This shows us something important about how translation relates to power. Translation errors, or mere differences, don't matter much in themselves. Their effects depend on how they are interpreted and used. Nevertheless, translations can reveal the pressures that have borne in on a negotiation, and the misunderstandings that have continued through it. One grammatically tiny but politically illuminating example occurs in United Nations Security Council Resolution 242 which was made in the wake of the 1967 Israeli-Arabic war. The English text requires 'withdrawal of Israeli armed forces from territories occupied in the recent conflict'. But the official French and unofficial Arabic versions have a definite article before 'territories': the meaning of those texts is closer to 'withdrawal of Israeli forces from the territories occupied in the recent conflict'. The difference has come into being partly for stylistic reasons: in Arabic (though not French) it would be odd to write this sort of phrase without a definite article. But there is a difference of meaning too. 'The territories' implies 'all the territories'; 'territories' suggests just some of them. Divergent aims and assumptions are made visible in these variants. The English is loose in a way that was probably deliberate in the circumstances. The other texts reveal a desire for a more stringent Resolution.

Delayed action

Translation differences can also have unexpected after-effects. One long-running example is the Treaty of Waitangi which was concluded between the British Crown and Maori chiefs of the North Island of New Zealand in 1840. This treaty is often cited as an instance of injustice facilitated through translation, and there is certainly truth in this view. The English text states that the Maori ceded 'sovereignty' to Queen Victoria whereas in the Maori text they give her *kawanatanga*, which is more like a governorship or protectorate. But the circumstances were complicated, and the subsequent history of the treaty has been surprising.

During the 1820s and 1830s the British government had no explicit ambition to establish a formal empire over New Zealand: a policy of 'minimum intervention' was maintained. However, by the late 1830s there were reports of violence being committed by settlers and dodgy land purchases being made by the private New Zealand Company. There was also a threat of incursion by France. So the British Colonial Secretary, Lord Normanby, sent an envoy, Captain William Hobson, to make a treaty with the Maori people that would enable New Zealand to be regulated by English law.

All the grindingly conflicting ideas of the well-meaning imperialist are visible in this initiative. Normanby seems to have felt genuine concern for the Maori people: he instructed Hobson that they 'must not be permitted to enter into any contracts in which they might be the ignorant and unintentional authors of injuries to themselves'. On the other hand, he took it for granted that Hobson, rather than any Maori, would be the best judge of what counted as 'injuries to themselves'. If they did not wish to submit to British sovereignty (for example) it would be Hobson's duty to persuade them to alter that wrong-headed view.

On top of these imperialist assumptions, the practical circumstances in New Zealand made full mutual understanding very difficult to achieve. The English text was translated by Reverend Henry Williams, the local head of the Church Missionary Society, who worked through the night with his son Edward to ready the treaty for an assembly of 500 Maori and 200 Pakeha (settlers) the next day. The written language that they were translating into was one that Williams had himself helped to establish. Before the advent of the first mission in 1814 Maori had been a wholly oral tongue. The missionaries had invented spellings and a written grammar so as to form a medium that the Bible and other Christian texts could be translated into; and then they taught the Maori people to read these books in this new writing.

This is how the Maori gained whatever understanding they had of Western ideas about government and land ownership. And so, as he translated the treaty of Waitangi, Williams must have been influenced by the religious translations that had been done before. *Kawanatanga* was a term that missionaries had themselves created from the pre-existing Maori word *kawa* which meant something like 'governor'; in their translation of the Bible they used it for the authority exercised by Pontius Pilate. Another word that Williams might have used for 'sovereignty' was *rangatiratanga* which meant something more like jurisdiction or chieftainship. But he chose to use this word to translate 'possession', that is the control that the Maori people would continue to have over their land.

Nonetheless, whichever Maori words had been chosen, there would still have been misunderstanding and cross-purposes. The key English terms in the treaty had distinctive meanings that derived from their use in English politics and law: they were locked into that particular community of interpretation. If *rangatirataga* and *kawanatanga* had swapped over, the Maori chiefs might have formed a better impression of the vigour of the British claim. But neither word could capture the peculiar combination of rights and duties embodied in the English conception of sovereignty.

Williams was not a lawyer and may not have understood the subtleties that were dropping out of his translation. Certainly, with the large assembly summoned for the next day, he will have been keen to produce a text that would go down well. Like Normanby and Hobson, he had a Christian and imperialist conviction that it was in the Maori people's best interests to sign the Treaty, whatever its precise terms. Finally he may have been influenced by the Maori view of the importance of oral explanation and agreement: during the negotiation it seems to have been Williams's spoken assurances that secured assent, more than a detailed analysis of the written language (as how could it not have been, with 700 people present and only one written document?) And so it was that, like Phaeneas two millennia before, Maori chiefs put their name to words whose meaning they did not fully grasp. One of them, Kaitaia Chief Napera Panakareao, gave his understanding of the Treaty in terms that correspond to something like this in English: 'the shadow of the land goes to Queen Victoria but the substance remains with us'. The English text of the Treaty said something rather different.

The translation differences in the Treaty of Waitangi reveal the misunderstandings between the two sides. Yet, just as with Phaeneas, they were not decisive when it came to what happened next. Over the ensuing decades, the British settlers put in place measures that progressively disempowered and dispossessed Maori people. They established a tax on land where crops were not being grown, with confiscation being the penalty for non-payment. They set up a system of self-government from which the Maori people were almost completely excluded. But they didn't appeal to the conflicted wording of the Treaty of Waitangi to enable them to do this: they simply had confidence in their superior power.

However, the Treaty did start to matter again in New Zealand politics in the 1970s. The Maori people were protesting against their dispossession of the land, and they used the Maori text of the Treaty of Waitangi, and its differences from the English, to build their argument. A tribunal was set up to enquire into injustices and some revisionary judgments have been made.

Translations can bow to power, and smooth the pathways of injustice. But when they do so, they make injustice visible. This means that, when the landscape of power, and therefore of interpretation, begins to alter, slips and differences in translation can be exploited. Translations can rise up against the authority they started out by serving.

Words of God

New Zealand was not the only place where English Bibles (themselves, of course, translations) were being translated into other languages. Many other missionaries, in many other countries, were trying to spread the good news via translation; and they are still doing it today. An American evangelical website claims that the Bible has been fully translated into 500 languages and partially into another 1,300; translation projects are apparently getting started in a further 2,300. It is an amazingly ambitious endeavour. Many of these languages were (or are) oral: in them, the Bible was (or will be) not only the first book ever translated, but the first written and printed book full stop.

When language is given letters and a written grammar for the sake of Bible translation, the results can be peculiar. In Malaysia, in the early 1800s, the writer Abdullah bin Abdul Kadir Munsyi came across Bible translations that had been done by the Dutch preacher and doctor Melchior Leydekker nearly a century before.

Leydekker had used first Roman and then Arabic letters to represent Malay speech. A skilled linguist, Abdullah found he could read the words easily, even though this was the first time he had seen Malay represented in print. But the punctuation and idiom felt wrong to him: 'it all sounded very clumsy to my ear, and I was inclined to say: "this is a book of the white man"'.

Nowadays, missionaries tend to be anxious to avoid the sort of awkwardness that troubled Abdullah bin Abdul Kadir Munsyi. The dominant theorist of missionary translation, Eugene Nida, recommends the use of anything that sounds natural in the receiving language, with the cultural and doctrinal specifics of the Bible text being downplayed accordingly. In the Bamabra language of West Africa, the English word 'redemption' should be translated with a term that literally means something like 'God took our heads out' (i.e. from the iron collar of slavery). In contemporary America, the phrase that appears in the King James Bible as 'salute one another with a holy kiss' should become 'give each other a hearty handshake all round'.

Missionaries can adopt this permissive practice of translation because they feel that their whole enterprise is divinely sanctioned. Their job is not so much to give readers a precise understanding of the holy text as to persuade them to join a community of believers. As one historian of the movement puts it: 'accessibility has been counted more significant than the distortion which goes with it', the reason being that translation of the Bible, however loose, 'has almost always resulted in net gain for people who wanted access to it' (the times when it did not produce 'net gain' are not explored).

But 'distortions'—or 'shifts', to use the more usual word—in Bible translations can matter hugely when they encapsulate differences in doctrine. The Baptist William Carey was a prolific translator of the Bible into Bengali, Sanskrit, and other Indian languages in Calcutta in the late 18th and early 19th centuries. But he incurred the hostility of the Anglican British and Foreign Bible Society because, in line with his belief in full body baptism, he used the word 'immerse' instead of 'baptise'.

In Macau and Canton, at roughly the same time, there was even controversy about how to translate the word 'God'. Roman Catholics had been instructed by the Pope to use '天主' (*Tiānzhǔ*—something like 'heavenly ruler') a word that was not tainted by association with Confucian, Daoist, or Buddhist beliefs, but which in consequence was familiar to rather few Chinese people. The presbyterian Robert Morrison preferred '神' (*Shén*), a popular generic name for a deity; but when his translation was revised in the mid-19th century to produce a composite protestant 'Union Version' the Confucian term '上帝' (*Shàngdi*)—meaning something like 'ancient lord'—was proposed instead. Advocates penned hundreds of pages of argument on each side, but consensus remained elusive. The upshot was that 'to this day there are *Shén* Christians and *Shàngdi* Christians as well as Catholic *Tiānzhǔ* Christians'—each group with its own translation.

This Chinese scenario reveals something fundamental about how translation has functioned in the history of Christianity. Each new translation has tended to be viewed as embodying the faith of the community it belongs to. It is granted the same sort of status as an original.

Holy books

For the Roman Catholic Church, from the middle ages onwards, this translation with the status of an original has been the Latin Bible known as the Vulgate, which was translated from the Hebrew and Greek source texts mainly by St Jerome in the late 4th century. Gradually vernacular translations started to be done too. How they were viewed depended on their context. The Church appears to have been quite happy with fragmentary or parallel text translations that were made as part of a process of monastic commentary. But stand-alone translations that looked like a challenge to the interpretive authority of the Church were more of a problem. In England, for instance, possession of any of the 14th-century translations of scripture done by William Wycliffe and his followers was punishable by death.

In the early 16th century, movements for reform of the Church, together with the rise in classical scholarship known as Humanism, created the conditions for new translations; and the new technology of print meant that they could be widely distributed. In the 1520s, Martin Luther was translating the Bible into German as part of the theological and institutional polemic that sparked the Protestant Reformation. Inspired by Luther, William Tyndale started a new English translation. The project was forbidden by the Bishop of London so Tyndale had to move to Hamburg and then Worms to carry it out.

When Tyndale's translation began to be published (it was done in parts, beginning with the New Testament), Thomas More attacked it on behalf of the authorities. What's interesting is that More focused not so much on mistakes in Tyndale's translation, as on his choice of different words from those that the Church community had got in the habit of using for its own beliefs and practices. Tyndale wrote 'favour', not 'grace'; 'love', not 'charity'; 'congregation', not 'church'; 'senior', not 'priest'; 'acknowledge', not 'confess'. When believers looked into Tyndale's Bible they would not find a blueprint for the established institutions of the Church, but rather something that pointed towards Protestant devotional practices.

Towards the end of the 16th century a group of Roman Catholic theologians bowed to the inevitable. They set about producing a translation that would embody the beliefs and habits of the Catholic community and would therefore differ markedly from Tyndale's and other Protestant and Anglican Bibles. In this translation, known as the Rheims–Douai Bible, there was not 'daily bread' but 'supersubstantial bread', not a 'Holy Ghost' but rather a 'Paraclete'. These choices are the opposite of those recommended by Eugene Nida. They make the Bible about as hard to understand for the everyday English reader as any translation could be while still being a translation. They embody the conviction that a priesthood is necessary to preserve and expound the meanings of these unusual, sacred words.

In all these cases, translation choices matter insofar as they respond to the beliefs of an interpretive community. It is the same principle that we saw at work in the translation of political treaties. The starkest instance is also the most famous translation choice in the history of the Bible: Luther's decision to write, in his translation of Romans 3.28, that people are justified not by works but by faith alone, *alleine durch den Glauben*.

The controversial word is *alleine*, 'alone'. It asserts that the route to salvation is not through good works, or good works animated by faith, but through faith alone. When he defended this translation, Luther made various points. He said that *alleine durch den Glauben* was everyday, idiomatic German: to leave out the *alleine* would make the phrase sound stilted. This is like the difference between 'territories' and 'the territories' in Security Council Resolution 242, as we saw in the last section. Luther also argued that his translation was in line with previous interpretations that had not attracted the ire of the Pope. And he was right. Even such an irreproachable Catholic authority as St Thomas Aquinas had inserted the Latin word corresponding to 'alone' in his translation of the phrase: *in sola fide*.

The difference lies in the contexts in which these translations appeared. Luther's phrase formed part of a challenge to the interpretive community of the Roman Catholic Church, and the endeavour to create different pathways of interpretation in its place.

Many translators of the Bible have recognized that a range of different versions can be a good thing. The translators of the King James Bible wrote in their preface that 'variety of translations is profitable for the finding out of the sense of the Scriptures'—yet, despite this, the Bible they had produced went on to become the sacred book of the Anglican Church. Its provisional status as a translation dropped away when it became established as the embodiment of a community's rituals and beliefs.

This state of affairs owes something to the technology of print for which these Bibles were produced. The King James translation was the book that was to be found in Anglican churches; believers who wanted their own Bibles might easily feel that one copy—one holy book—was enough. Nowadays, websites make it easy to compare numerous different texts, helping Christians to see that any given version is not in itself the word of God, but just one translation.

This is in fact how translation has always been understood in the Muslim world—so the technology of print is not the whole explanation. It is often thought that translation of the Qur'an is forbidden, but this is not the case. From the earliest days of Islam, the Qur'an was interpreted and explained via translations which might be spoken, written in manuscript, or (eventually) printed. For instance, there were several famous early translations into Persian. What is different is how these translations were—and are—presented and understood.

Each translation does not become a new sacred text: a translation cannot be 'The Qur'an' in the way that a translation can be 'The Bible'. Rather, translations are seen as helps towards understanding the sacred text which remains in Arabic. They are typically interlineated with the words Muhammad wrote, or printed in parallel text. In this way of seeing things, translations do not take the place of their source text; they point towards it. They cannot in themselves take on the status of 'the word of God'; instead, they show how it might be interpreted in other, human words.

Suffering censorship

The English Church and State authorities didn't like Tyndale's Bible translation. As soon as its publication began in the 1520s they set about suppressing it. Booksellers were banned from stocking it; copies found were burnt. Eventually, Tyndale too was hunted down and burnt like his book (though the translation was not quite the whole reason—he had also criticized Henry VIII's divorce plans).

In 1991 another translator was murdered, stabbed repeatedly in the neck and face. He was Hitoshi Igarashi, the Japanese translator of Salman Rushdie's novel *The Satanic Verses* which had offended some Muslims and provoked the Iranian leader Ayatollah Khomeini to order the killing of anyone involved in its publication. Igarashi's murderer (who has not been brought to justice) must have felt he was carrying out the Ayatollah's command; it also led to attacks on Rushdie's Italian translator Ettore Capriolo and Norwegian publisher Milliam Nygaard.

Of course any book can be met with hostility. And any book can be censored. But translations have always had a particular tendency to provoke sensitive audiences and oppressive authorities because they bring in ideas from outside. These days, when dictatorial régimes such as Saudi Arabia's put content filters on the internet, they also have to ban translation apps such as Google Translate because these can be used to circumvent the filters.

In Nazi Germany, translations were subjected to fiercer censorship than all home-grown texts except for political writing. In Franco's Spain, by contrast, translations went through the same system as everything else, which meant they had to be screened for their attitudes to religious belief, morals, the Church, and the régime.

But the censors still tended to bite most harshly at translations because the Spanish public had a worrying appetite for American culture. Sometimes the results were bizarre. In the 1948 film *Arch of Triumph*, a character played by Ingrid Bergman has relationships with various men to whom she isn't married. But not according to the dubbed Spanish dialogue. At one point, she is asked if the man she is with is her husband. Bergman shakes her head—at the same time as her dubbed Spanish voice says, 'Sí' ('Yes').

In 1966, Franco's régime introduced what appeared to be a softening of the censorship rules. Publishers no longer had to submit all texts to the censors before publication but only the ones they chose. However, this change of procedure did not in fact improve the situation; on the contrary. If a book turned out to offend the authorities after it had been published it would have to be pulped—an expensive business. And the publishers might be thought to be partners in the crime. So, on the whole, they became very careful not to publish anything displeasing to the régime—perhaps even more careful than the censors themselves would have been.

This interesting fact shows us something crucial about the way censorship operates. It is never a matter of a single oppressive agency simply banning or cutting texts which 'the people' would unanimously love to be able to read. Rather, different individuals are complicit, accepting or resistant to varying degrees; propaganda can make them internalize the State's demands even if they don't agree with them, or they can find themselves having to make the best of a difficult situation. Censorship is therefore a complex, permeating web of psychological pressure and misinformation as well as explicit rules.

In Mussolini's Italy, in the 1930s, the novelist and translator Elio Vittorini, who was working for the publisher Mondadori, suggested cuts to D. H. Lawrence's novel *St Mawr* to suit Fascist tastes. He felt it necessary to engage in censorship himself before the official censors did—this, at a time when his own fiction was also being censored. In Nazi Germany there was no official index of prohibited books because booksellers were expected to know from their own 'healthy instinct' which books might damage the *Volk*. That is to say, they too were expected to work as censors.

Censorship almost always acts against some sections of the population more than others. Back in the 16th century, royals, aristocrats, and Church dignitaries could quite happily own translated Bibles which ordinary people would be punished for possessing. In Victorian Britain, translations were at risk of being prosecuted for obscenity whereas foreign-language texts were not. In 1888, for instance, the publisher Ernest Vizetelly was taken to court for printing English versions of novels by Émile Zola, even though he had taken the precaution of Bowdlerizing them in advance, and even though the French originals could circulate without restriction. The reason seems to have been that only the uneducated were felt to be at risk from Zola's immoral influence. Readers who knew French were likely to be good chaps who could be trusted to keep up appearances. Either that, or they were already corrupted beyond repair.

Another way of circumventing Victorian censorship was to print your book in an expensive private edition, thus ensuring that only the privileged could read it. This is how Sir Richard Burton had got away with his gloriously salacious translation of the *Arabian Nights* in 1885.

This sort of complexity in the workings of censorship creates particular expressive possibilities for authors and translators. Under Stalin, Anna Akhmatova and Osip Mandelstam developed hermetic styles of poetry which, to the astute reader, implied more than they could be proven to say; Eugenio Montale did something similar in Mussolini's Italy. In 17th-century England John Dryden and other writers used translation as a shield for political views which they would not have been able to express openly. Dryden, as a Catholic, thought that the Crown should have followed the Stuart line of succession, and that the Protestants William and Mary were usurpers. When, in his translation of the *Aeneid*, he writes that the leadership of Rome was handed down by 'sure succession' the contrast would have seemed pointed to the knowing reader. But if Dryden were ever challenged he could lay the blame on Virgil.

Once you see that censorship permeates literary taste and affects the styles of authors and translators, you can notice continuities between cultures that are censored and those we think of as being free. Of course, censorship by governments or violent groups is a particular, abhorrent practice; but still, authors and translators in any culture write with an awareness of what their readers and the literary authorities are likely to want. A text that is felt to be objectionable can be sunk by bad reviews, or simply never published. This means that all translators have to develop something of the same awareness as Dryden and Vittorini, negotiating between what the culture will accept and what they might otherwise have liked to write. As we saw in Chapter 1, all translation is diplomatic translation. Translators have a responsibility to represent the distinctive qualities of the text they are translating, however challenging it might be. They also have a responsibility to enable it to be read.

The burden of translation

For help in defining their responsibilities, translators can turn to their professional associations, many of which publish codes of conduct. One question that features in several of these codes is what should happen if someone thinks a text they have been asked to translate will be used for illegal or dishonest purposes. The Irish Translators' and Interpreters' Association (ITIA), for one, states that translators should refuse to take on any such work. This sort of rule recognizes the important truth that translators are not humanoid machines who simply accomplish a technical function. They are people who make choices and therefore have responsibility for what they do.

However, strangely, when the task of translation itself is under way, the translator's agency and responsibility appear to shrink. Here is the ITIA code again: 'members of the Association shall endeavour to the utmost of their ability to provide a guaranteed faithful rendering of the original text which must be entirely free of their own personal interpretation, opinion or influence'. Yet, as we saw in Chapter 4, every translation includes an element of personal interpretation which can be exercised more or less freely according the genre of the source text and the purpose of the translation.

Even when translators have very little freedom indeed, they are still involved in their work as people. Primo Levi gives the example of a Jewish German forced to act as an interpreter in a Nazi concentration camp:

> Si vedono le parole non sue, le parole cattive, torcergli la bocca uscendo, come se sputasse un boccone disgustoso
>
> [You could see the words that were not his, the horrible words, twisting his mouth as they came out, as though he were spitting out a disgusting mouthful]

If you were asked to translate Hitler's *Mein Kampf*, you might also want to find some way of distancing yourself from the words that are coming into English through your writing. For example, an introduction and footnotes could make it clear that you are presenting the book for a critical reading, not expecting it to be agreed with.

The ITIA's rule might apply fairly well to a situation where the source is neutral and the translation's purpose is clearly defined—for instance a business document being translated for an international company, or a medical textbook for an academic publisher. In this sort of case, a translator's choices are strictly limited by agreed norms. But more complex texts give translators greater room for choice and therefore require them to shoulder more responsibility.

Take for instance Mahasweta Devi, a Bengali writer whose fiction explores violence against women, among other kinds of oppression. Devi's work has been translated into English by Gayatri Chakravorty Spivak who explains that she tried to 'surrender to the text' in order to represent as much as she could of its stylistic and political challenge. But Leela Sarkar, Devi's translator into Malayalam, the language of Kerala in south India, did not feel able to act in the same way. Feminism is not as powerful in Kerala as in the Anglophone West, and so Sarker chose to soften some of Devi's harder hitting scenes. In one moment from a violent confrontation in Devi's story 'Draupadi', Spivak translates: 'She looks around and chooses the front of Senanayak's white shirt to spit a bloody gob at.' In Sarkar's Malayalam translation, everything after the word 'around' has been left out.

We can't judge the rights and wrongs of this decision without more knowledge of the circumstances in which it was made. But what we can see is that Leela Sarkar made a choice, and did so in the context of multiple responsibilities: to the source text and its author; to potential readers; to her publisher; and to herself. Given the language she felt able to use, in the context for which she was writing, Sarkar decided that the best translation choice was to cut those words. Here again, just as with Elio Vittorini in Fascist Italy (see the previous section) or the *dragoman* who was polite to Elizabeth I (see Chapter 1), it is crucial to realize that translation is never just into 'a language', but rather into a particular kind of language, in particular circumstances, for particular purposes.

This means that even in very regulated situations—even the ones that the ITIA's code fits best—there can still be a distinctly personal element of imaginativeness and sensitivity in finding the right kind of language for the given context. Think of an interpreter mediating between a vulnerable person such as an immigrant and an authoritative institution like a law court (a situation I have touched on already in Chapter 4). The interpreter will need not only to be 'faithful' to what the person says, in the sense of putting it into the English language, but also tuned in to the circumstances so as to get the testimony across with sufficient accuracy in an appropriate style.

This is why skilled translators are crucial to the just functioning of legal and social services. If there is no suitably qualified interpreter for a court case, the hearing will be cancelled. With social services, the responsibility of translation is likely to fall on someone who shouldn't have to bear it. A poem-memoir by Rabia Rehmen, a British Pakistani teenager at school in Oxford, makes the point vividly:

Sitting in a small room with a desk and three chairs. I'm suffocated already.
Being interviewed by a short grumpy lady in glasses too big for her small face.
Her badge is upside down hanging on her blue dress. She didn't even greet us.
It's important to pay attention. I have to maintain my friendly tone—I have to!
I translate for my mum. She doesn't speak English. If it weren't for me, there would be no meeting. They can't afford translators, anymore.
I'm never paid, but it's still my duty.
Going to school isn't an excuse. This isn't fair.

Social services in the UK, Italy, and elsewhere increasingly make similar demands on interpreters who are neither trained nor paid.

Powerful choices

A translator's choices can promote one way of using a language over another. Imagine that you had to translate the title of Jacob Bronowski's 1973 TV series 'The Ascent of Man'. Sensitivities to gendered terms have shifted since the 1970s: if the series were being remade today it would have to be called something different. But how would you remake the title in another language? You might feel that you want to be historically authentic, and preserve the gender prejudice by choosing similar, 1970s-style terms. Or you might want to translate the title into contemporary language that feels more your own—perhaps the equivalent of something like 'The Development of the Human'.

If you made the first choice, you might want to be sure that it's clear from the context that you have not used your own words but rather ones you feel to be historically appropriate. This would be the case if, say, the title were appearing in a nostalgic box-set of 'TV series of the 70s'. If you made the second choice, you might want to add a footnote giving a more literal translation of the title. This move would make it visible that the language is changing, and that your translation choices are helping to make the change happen.

Decisions of this kind tend to be particularly charged when they have to do with gender and sexuality. In Lesotho, in southern Africa, women can develop intense friendships with other women which can co-exist happily with marriage even though they involve sexual intimacy. The Sesotho term for this sort of relationship is *motsoalle*. How could we translate it? The word 'lesbian' would bring with it a set of assumptions that don't fit this context, while 'very special friend', the phrase chosen by one translator, sounds twee. Perhaps the best solution would be to use the Sesotho term with an explanatory footnote, thereby making it possible for a new word, naming a new aspect of gender identity and sexuality, to come into English.

New words, expressing new ways of being—among many other kinds of novelty—come into languages all the time; and translation helps this to happen. In the Arabic of the Maghreb, the words for describing homosexuality traditionally distinguished between active and passive sexual roles, with the passive being viewed pejoratively. But then a new term, *mithli* came into being to express a more reciprocal style of homosexual identity, roughly equivalent to the Anglo-American word 'gay'. *Mithli* includes the idea of 'same' and was probably influenced by translation from the French *homo*.

It is sometimes said that translators have a responsibility to give a strong impression of the linguistic particularity, or 'otherness' of the source text. This view has roots in work by the German philosopher Friedrich Schleiermacher in the 19th century, and was elaborated by the French literary critic Antoine Berman in the 1980s; it has since been popularized in the Anglophone world by the translation theorist Lawrence Venuti. But the value of a 'foreignizing' style of translation is always dependent on context. To bring the word *motsoalle* into English is to foreignize—and that seems necessary. But to Leela Sarkar in Kerala or to the *dragoman* writing to Elizabeth I, it was more important to produce a text that would not offend their readers. Translators' responsibilities pull in different directions, and they feel the pressure of competing powers.

Chapter 6
Words in the world

Translation happens everywhere all the time. Anyone can find different words for something that has been said in another language, or in the same one; anyone with internet access can click the 'translate' option on their browser. But when it comes to the public and commercial world of printed books, political documents, diplomatic negotiations, business transactions, and world news, translation is strictly limited. Official rules and market forces combine to determine who can do it, how it is done, and which languages it involves. In these international structures there is less violence and less scope for resistance than in the power struggles I explored in the previous chapter. But in fact it is here that translation and power are most intimately intertwined.

The book trade

Take the international market for printed books. Completely accurate data are impossible to assemble: UNESCO's *Index Translationum* attempts to cover a hundred countries between 1979 and 2009, but the entries are patchy; many States maintain their own records, but they are scattered and hard to compare. So only broad-brush conclusions can be reached. But they are striking. Of all the books translated in the world, about 40 per cent were originally written in English (including American and world

Englishes). Add three more languages—French, German, and Russian—and you have the origin of three-quarters of all translated books anywhere (though the prominence of Russian has declined somewhat since the collapse of the USSR in 1991).

The next most translated languages are each the source of between 1 and 3 per cent of all translated texts. They are Italian, Spanish, Swedish, Japanese, Danish, Latin, Dutch, ancient Greek, and Czech. They sit on the upper slopes of a gradual decline which ends with barely translated languages such as Ahom, Lushootseed, and Tok Pisin. On the way you pass Chinese, Arabic, and Portuguese in sixteenth, seventeenth, and eighteenth places, with Hindi further down in forty-fifth. These are among the most commonly spoken languages in the world and yet they generate comparatively few translations.

The cultures that give the most translated books to the world receive rather few by comparison. The figures are usually expressed as percentages of the total numbers of books published in those countries. So, in the United States and the United Kingdom, fewer than 3 per cent of books published are translations, while in France and Germany the figure is between 10 and 12 per cent. In Greece, by contrast, translations account for 40 per cent of the total number of books published. Given these percentages, the obvious reaction is: how open-minded the Greeks are! How xenophobic the British and Americans!

However, the real picture is more complicated. No doubt it would be better if more, and more varied, books were translated into English. But the main reason why the percentage for the United Kingdom and United States looks so low is that the total number of books published in each county is very large. In the UK about 180,000 books are published each year. If 2.5 per cent of those are translations, the actual number of translated books will be about 4,500. In Germany, about 82,000 books are published, and in France about 42,000; 10 per cent of those numbers gives 8,200 and 4,200 translated books, respectively. In Greece, about 7,000 books are published—40 per cent of that is 2,800. So the actual number of books translated into each language does not vary nearly as much as the percentages. If you simply count the books, English speakers are not that hostile to translations after all.

There are two other important truths that are thrown into relief by these figures. The first is that the sort of translation engaged in by publishers, and measured by the *Index Translationum*, is only one of the many kinds of translation that take place round the world. It is 'Translation Rigidly Conceived', in the terms we developed in Chapter 2: a process which creates equivalence between texts in separate, standard, written languages, each typically supported by a State.

The second is that this sort of translation, as it is done to books, is heavily centred in Western Europe and North America: about 40 per cent of the global print translation of books takes place in a merry-go-round between English, German, and French.

But 'Translation Rigidly Conceived' is not the only sort of trans-linguistic activity that books can be involved in. According to the *Index Translationum*, the amount of translation in and out of India, and in and out of China, is fairly small. But the way languages exist in those countries is different from in the West. In India there are fifty languages that have more than a million speakers each, and many other local languages and dialects. China is even more multilingual, with the added complication that many mutually unintelligible spoken languages share the same written script. A vast amount of translation happens within these countries, in forms and media that are beneath the radar of the *Index Translationum*, including oral re-telling and writing that is not bound in books.

The trade routes of translated books reveal a cultural hegemony centred in North America and Western Europe. Like many hegemonies, it has good aspects as well as bad: the massive publication of English books in England is a sign of cultural energy as much as of resistance to the foreign. But this energy is channelled through a particular cultural system—a particular set of ways of using language and putting it into books. 'Translation Rigidly Conceived' is part of that same system.

As Western cultures evolve there are two kinds of change involving translation that might happen. The first is, simply, that more books from more languages might be translated. This is what people interested in translation typically campaign for at the moment.

The second is that the assumptions and practices of 'Translation Rigidly Conceived' might themselves begin to shift. There might be more plural modes of translation that release the multiple possible meanings of the source text rather than offering just one equivalent (I call this 'Prismatic Translation'). Other modes might mix languages—rather like *kanbun-kundoku*—instead of jumping from a standardized version of one language to a standardized version of another. There might be more translation into varied styles and dialects. There are signs that all this is beginning to happen, but there has been less talk of why, and to what end. Europe's national cultures are shifting under the pressures of immigration and emigration, both human and cultural. They are becoming more fluidly multilingual, more aware of the thickness and variety of language use. There is a tension between these developments and the structure of 'Translation Rigidly Conceived'. Translation is in essence a tolerant and exploratory activity, less regulatory than enriching. This aspect of it should be helped to flourish.

Official channels

Multinational political organizations, such as the United Nations and the institutions of the European Union, generate a vast amount of translation. The European Parliament alone employs about 330 permanent interpreters, with another 1,800 freelancers who can be called on at peak times. And that is just interpreters: reams of written documents have to be translated too. Yet, in these institutions, just as with the book trade, translation does as much to regulate the use of language as to multiply it.

The United Nations routinely works in six official languages—Arabic, Chinese, English, French, Russian, and Spanish—with many documents also being translated into German. Already in this case there are $7 \times 6 = 42$ different possible language pairs to cope with. But the European Parliament is substantially more polyglot, with twenty-four offical languages. That means 552 possible pairs. It is as much a logistical as a linguistic challenge.

The Parliament meets this challenge partly via the practice of relay interpreting, which makes use of an intermediary language, typically English. This means that you don't have to have someone who can interpret directly between (say) Polish and Portuguese: if one person can handle Polish into English, and another English into Portuguese, then the job can be done.

It is also the case that the European Parliament is not as polyglot in practice as in theory. The Commission, which prepares the legislation, works only in French, German, and English, and the Commissioners speak in English when they present matters to Parliament. Many MEPs follow suit and use English—often their second language—to respond. The result is that less interpretation is needed than at first seems likely. English dominates, while some other languages are hardly used at all. In the entirety of the Parlimentary discussion that took place during 2012, for instance, Latvian, Maltese, and Estonian were each spoken for no more than one hour each.

And of course none of the myriad 'non-offical' languages and dialects of Europe—Manx, Bresà, Roma, Vote, Pite Saami,

Karaim, Istriot, etc., etc.—are used at all. The legislative machine requires standard national languages that can be lined up, via translation and intepretation, into reliable patterns of equivalence. Otherwise debaters would miss each other in a jungle of expressive mis-comprehension, and European laws would mean different things in different places.

So in multinational political institutions, just like the international book trade, translation tends to reinforce standard national languages, together with the dominance of English as both a national language and an international lingua franca. Translation helps to maintain this structure; and this structure in its turn makes translation easier than it would otherwise be.

This is not the only way in which the workings of language are restricted in multinational political institutions. Debate and legislation do not exploit all the resources of even the small set of standard national languages that they use. There are lots of things that it is possible to say in a national language that do not usually get said in European Parliamentary debates, let alone legislation—for instance: 'the skip coughed and the thrower dumped the handle' or 'sweet dreams my love' or 'that'll be two pounds fifty'.

A language is not a flat plain of grammar and words. It is ridged and valleyed into kinds of usage. None of us is fluent in every aspect of the languages we think we know; all of us are at home in some bits more than others. The kinds of language used in multinational political institutions are more limited still. They are limited by register, which means the language appropriate to the subject, for example agriculture or migration; and they are limited by genre, which means what the language is being used to do, for example make a speech or lay down a law. It matters that translators and interpreters know they will not have to turn any old bit of Bulgarian into Finnish but rather a statement about fisheries in Bulgarian into a statement about fisheries in Finnish.

Only a subsection of each language will have to be used. This is crucial for oral interpreters who have to translate almost instantaneously. They can work up the expected subject matter and register for a debate before it starts, storing up pre-prepared chunks of translation; and they can draw on parallel databases of key legislative terms.

United Nations resolutions have a distinctive structure and vocabulary (see Box 1).

Box 1 A United Nations resolution

A/RES/59/35 Resolution adopted by the General Assembly [on the report of the Sixth Committee (A/59/505)] 59/35. Responsibility of States for internationally wrongful acts

The General Assembly,

Recalling its resolution 56/83 of 12 December 2001, the annex to which contains the text of the articles on responsibility of States for internationally wrongful acts,

Emphasizing the continuing importance of the codification and progressive development of international law, as referred to in Article 13, paragraph 1 (a), of the Charter of the United Nations,

Noting that the subject of responsibility of States for internationally wrongful acts is of major importance in relations between States,

1. Commends once again the articles on responsibility of States for internationally wrongful acts to the attention of Governments, without prejudice to the question of their future adoption or other appropriate action;

2. Requests the Secretary-General to invite Governments to submit their written comments on any future action regarding the articles;

3. Also requests the Secretary-General to prepare an initial compilation of decisions of international courts, tribunals and other bodies referring to the articles and to invite Governments to submit information on their practice in this regard, and further requests the Secretary-General to submit this material well in advance of its sixty-second session;

4. Decides to include in the provisional agenda of its sixty-second session the item entitled 'Responsibility of States for internationally wrongful acts'. 65th plenary meeting 2 December 2004

There is a Preamble, which has a prescribed grammatical structure, and which has to start with a signpost such as: 'Acknowledging', 'Affirming', 'Alarmed', 'Approving', 'Aware', 'Bearing in mind', 'Being convinced', 'Cognizant that', 'Concerned by', 'Deeply disturbed by', 'Desiring', 'Determined that', 'Encouraged by', 'Fully aware', 'Guided by', 'Having considered', 'Mindful that', 'Noting with approval', 'Noting with regret', 'Recalling', 'Recognizing', 'Regretting'—and so on.

Once the scene has been set, the 'operative' part of the resolution cuts in. It too has a set grammatical structure and way of beginning: 'Accepts', 'Adopts', 'Affirms', 'Appeals', 'Appreciates', 'Decides', 'Declares', 'Deplores', 'Emphasizes', 'Encourages', 'Notes', 'Reaffirms', 'Recognizes', 'Recommends', 'Regrets', 'Approves', 'Authorizes', 'Calls upon', 'Concurs', 'Condemns', 'Confirms', 'Congratulates', 'Considers', 'Endorses', 'Expresses its appreciation', 'Expresses its conviction', 'Expresses its regret', 'Expresses its sympathy', 'Expresses its thanks', 'Expresses the hope', 'Reiterates', 'Suggests', 'Supports', 'Takes note of', 'Urges', and 'Welcomes'.

Each of these formulae has well-worn counterparts in the United Nation's other tongues. Interpreters and translators in multinational political institutions have to move nimbly between languages; but at least they have the fixed stepping-stones of register and genre to support them.

The highways of global news

Global news also has its official channels; and here too powerful standard languages combine with conventions of genre and register to create an efficient, exclusive translation structure. Many newspapers have their own foreign correspondents; there are also various fluid, citizen-led pathways which I will explore further later. But the international motorway network of news is maintained by three dominant agencies: Reuters, Agence France Presse (AFP), and Associated Press.

These agencies are rooted, respectively, in Britain, France, and the United States; their global reach was established with the spread of the telegraph in the 19th and early 20th centuries. The languages through which they allow news to circulate are determined by this heritage. Reuters and AFP use English, French, Spanish, Portuguese, and Arabic (this last being added in the mid-20th century). Associated Press offers the same selection, only with Dutch instead of Portuguese.

Mainstream global news, then, is communicated through about the same number of languages as the political deliberations of the United Nations; and there is a two-thirds overlap between the two sets of channels. But the practice of translation is quite different in each case. The United Nations maintains teams of specialized translators and interpreters, as we have seen. However, in news agencies, reporters and editors need to be able to translate for themselves. Translation happens at every stage of the construction of an international news story, from interviews on the ground to editing in the office.

For instance, a 2006 Reuters story about fighting between Israel and Hezbollah draws on Israeli and Lebanese sources. They may have spoken in Arabic and Hebrew and been translated, either by the reporter or an intermediary; or they may have been using English as a second language. The story was then written up in English and sent round the world. Here is the first paragraph:

> Hizbollah fought fierce battles with Israeli troops on the Lebanese border on Thursday, as thousands more foreigners fled the nine-day-old war in Lebanon, including 1,000 Americans evacuated by US Marines.

In Reuters's Spanish office, the evacuation of Americans seemed less interesting than it probably would have done to the English-speaking readership of the original story. So the Spanish editor re-wrote the paragraph as he translated it, substituting a different detail: that the United Nations Secretary General Kofi Annan had called for a cessation of hostilities. The Spanish version also altered the dynamics of the first part of the sentence: now it is 'Israel' that fought fierce battles with Hezbollah ('Israel mantuvo el jueves fuertes enfrentamientos militares con Hezbolá') rather than Hezbollah that fought with 'Israeli troops'. This shift subtly re-directs a reader's sympathies, presenting the State of Israel, rather than Hezbollah, as the aggressor, and Hezbollah, rather than individual Israelis, as being under attack (notice also how 'troops', in the English version, sounds approving, whereas a word like 'fighters' would not have done).

Translation in global news is dominated by the idea of the 'story'. The story consists of those aspects of an event that will appeal to the target readership. The journalist on the ground searches for the makings of a story. Translation and interpreting are vital enablers of this search. But difficulties and changes in translation, together with the differences of understanding that they reveal, tend to be overlooked in the heat of the chase.

At the editing stage too, the idea of the story determines which bits of the incoming report are selected for translation, and in what way. Genre and register are important here just as in the

United Nations: it matters that the editor is translating, not just from English into Spanish, but from the register of political conflict and genre of news report in English into the equivalent Spanish register and genre. But, unlike the United Nations translator, the Reuters editor has liberty to re-shape a given text to suit a new readership in the new language. The process is sometimes called 'trans-editing', not translation.

Trans-editing reveals ideological shifts that play some part in all translation but are especially marked in the translation of news. To report a news event in a given language is to frame it in a world view, to adapt it to a set of perspectives and assumptions. The highways of global news don't just transport stories from one place to another. They determine what counts as news, and fix the angles it can be viewed from.

Machines, rules, and statistics

As we have seen, translation is never simply from one language to another. It is always from a subset of one language to a subset of another: not just French into English but a conversation about fashion in French into a conversation about fashion in English. Just like an interpreter at the United Nations, we can guess the kinds of words and phrases that are likely to crop up in this subset of language because any conversation re-deploys elements of conversations that have been had before. To a surprising degree, using language means repeating previous uses of language. And translation involves translating language that, somewhere or other, has probably already been translated. This fact is crucial to the way computers do translation.

The hope that computers might be made to translate goes back pretty much to their invention. Early efforts concentrated on writing programs to analyse the sentence structure and vocabulary of one language so that it could be converted, via a series of rules, into another. The results were often comprehensible but rarely fluent. Here is an example of machine translation from Russian in the 1970s:

> A contemporary airport is the involved complex of engineer constructions and techniques, for arrangement of which the territory, measured sometimes is required by thousands of hectares (for example the Moscow Airport Domodedovo, Kennedy's New York Airport).

It took a human being to re-write this into readable English:

> The modern airport is an elaborate complex of engineering structures and technical devices requiring a large territory, which, in some cases, measures thousands of hectares (for instance, Domodedovo Airport in Moscow or Kennedy Airport in New York).

At about the turn of the millennium, a wholly different approach gained ground. It started from the perception that a vast amount of translation already done by humans could be lined up with the source texts so that a computer could search them concurrently. Bilingual corpora like the English and French records of the Canadian Parliament or parallel text editions of Dante took on new significance. They were absorbed into databases that work like massive multilingual dictionaries not only of individual words but of sentences and turns of phrase.

In this method of translation, the computer does not apply rules for converting one language into another. It searches for all the ways a given phrase, and ones like it, have been translated in the past; and then it uses statistical techniques to determine which of the possibilities is likely to work best in the given context. Looking at the example from the 1970s, a modern statistical program is unlikely to come up with 'measured sometimes is required by thousands of hectares' because no human will have written that combination of words, or anything much like it, before.

The more text the computer can search the better. This means that common language pairs like French to English are much easier for a computer to translate than unusual ones like Portuguese to Tajik where there is little if any translation history to draw on. In these cases, computers can use relay translation—just like the United Nations—and deploy a mixture of rule-based and statistical techniques. All the same, a new-style translation of unusual language pairs is likely to be no better—and perhaps worse—than the old-style translation of Russian into English.

Even the not very unusual pairing of Chinese and English presents some difficulties. Here is a guest review from the travel website Tripadvisor, put into English by the leading statistically based program Google Translate:

> In Lanzhou, Jinjiang position better than the Mandarin and Crowne Plaza. Just a little old facilities, service is not dominant. Breakfast overslept, no experience. The hotel's transportation is convenient, although near the noisy area, probably because of the high floors medial, still relatively quiet. The hotel's free Wi-Fi off, less effective.

This English is probably a bit easier to understand than the 1970s account of the 'contemporary airport'. But the more interesting difference is in the kind of non-fluency that the two passages exhibit. The raw 1970s translation had nothing idiomatic about it at all: human intervention was needed to make it sound like English. But this Google translation has patches of fluency: 'just a little', 'probably because of', 'still relatively quiet'. You can see the program drawing on and re-using its human sources. It just hasn't yet got enough to go on to be able to stitch them together perfectly.

The biggest difference between statistical and rule-based approaches to translation is that statistical programs can get better by themselves. Every time you correct a translation in Google

Translate the program takes account of it; exercises done in language-learning apps like Duolingo feed machine translation—in fact every time a translation of anything is digitized or made available online a computer can suck it into itself to influence its future choices.

This extraordinary technology is advancing at speed. While it does so, it is radically changing our relationship to language. It enables communication where it was not possible before. And it is exposing people to strange versions of languages they thought they knew. Take 'Breakfast overslept, no experience'. You can see what it is getting at; but you can also enjoy it as a piece of language. It has a kind of poetry.

Memories, localization, and cyborgs

Multinational companies need translation. But the way programs like Google Translate gobble up text creates a problem of information security. So multinationals typically use software that works in a similar fashion but keeps their documents private. They also employ 'Translation Memories', comparatively small parallel corpora that show how particular kinds of text—or parts of the same long text—have already been translated, and make suggestions as a new translation is being done. And they maintain terminology databases to ensure that key words are always translated in the same way.

One reason why multinationals need translation is that consumers prefer to shop in places that seem familiar. Localization is the process by which a company adapts its web presence so that it looks at home wherever it is operating. This involves not only translating the language but also the design and functionality of a website: whether the text goes left to right or right to left or top to bottom; how dates are handled; how items are sorted in non-alphabetical languages; how the whole environment looks and feels. The need for comprehensive localization of this kind shows that language is continuous with habits of behaviour and non-verbal communication.

Another factor is of course the need for employees with different languages to be able to communicate with one another. Distinct modes of translation suit the various requirements. A good deal of human expertise is likely to have to go into the initial localization of a website. But once it has been set up, machine translation is likely to be able to handle communication channels like web-forms or live-chat technical support where the language will probably be simple and the topics predictable.

A company report, though, is likely to be translated by a human being working in conjunction with a Translation Memory and perhaps other computerized resources. A cyborg translator, then: part human, part machine. These days, professional translators almost always work in this way. And you can too. All you need to do is put some foreign text into Google Translate, receive a semi-English version like 'breakfast overslept, no experience' and complete the translation by understanding it to mean 'I overslept so cannot comment on the breakfast'. We are all becoming cyborg translators.

Crowds, bootleg trails, and glocal languages

Of course the internet does not just connect people to machines. It also connects people to other people, meaning that groups of human translators can be assembled virtually to work on a shared project. Some commercial translation services operate in this way; but the more interesting uses of crowd translation occur when it is done by volunteers. Anyone with the necessary language skills can translate a page from one of Wikipedia's websites to another, or contribute to the localization of the virtual reality environment, Second Life.

Crowds of citizen translators, working out of conviction and not for pay, can make information circulate beyond the official channels of international news agencies. One website, Global Voices, draws on more than 800 writers and translators, mainly volunteers, to give prominence to stories from around the world that might otherwise be missed, translating them into thirty languages. Global Voices originated in Harvard University but other uses of citizen translation are more embattled. Mosireen is a collective that filmed and publicized the events of the Egyptian revolution of 2011 and has continued to document the subsequent repression. It relies on volunteers to subtitle its videos.

So crowd translation creates unofficial 'bootleg trails', allowing people to access information that otherwise would not reach them. It also spreads awareness of translation difficulties, and of tactics for overcoming them. Wikipedia explains the sort of translation it is after: edit where necessary; explain terms that the new audience might not understand; use standard encyclopaedic style. TED, the storehouse of video-talks about ideas, teaches volunteers how to subtitle: use clear language, keep reading speed under twenty-one characters per second, break the lines in sensible places, be courteous to your crowd-collaborator. Translation is becoming a more conscious and visible part of the way more people use language.

This has some exhilarating consequences. Japanese manga animations have lots of fans. They get hold of the videos by semi-legal means and subtitle them in English so they can reach a larger audience. It's called 'fansubbing'. Because they love the material, and because they have the liberty of being amateurs, the fansubbers can innovate in ways that official subtitlers would find hard—though, unfortunately, the dubious copyright status of their work means I am unable to reproduce any examples in this book. In a frame from one manga, a teacher stands in front of a blackboard covered in Japanese characters: the English translations are arranged vertically on the blackboard too. In another, small writing at the top of the screen comments on a bit of wordplay that can't be captured in the main subtitle. Both tactics rely on intense involvement in the manga, to the point of feeling shared ownership. The fansubbers intervene in parts of the shot normally reserved for the original artwork, and they write their own impressions into the video itself.

These innovative practices arise because manga fansubbers form a community with shared desires and assumptions. They may be spread around the world but there is still a feeling of locality, of self-government, about their behaviour: they feel they have the liberty to depart from the usual conventions of translation in order to express what matters to them.

Words of Women from the Egyptian Revolution is another media activist group like Mosireen. Like the fansubbers, it adopts a translation practice that is in line with its beliefs. When the videos are subtitled in Spanish, the structure of that language would normally enforce gender distinctions: a 'friend', for instance, would have to be either a feminine 'amiga' or masculine 'amigo'. But this is at odds both with the Egyptian Arabic spoken by the women and with the conception of gender identity that they wish to present. So the subtitlers borrow a tactic from Spanish feminists and replace the prejudicial 'a' or 'o' with a neutral 'x'.

There is more that translators could do to throw into relief the friction between the energies of the Arab Spring and established habits of translation. A conference in Cairo in 2015 underlined the differences between key terms from the revolution and the English words that only roughly correspond to them, and between the Western connotations of the word 'democracy' and the similar but also different sort of civil society that the activists were trying to bring into being. But what the examples of Words of Women and the manga fansubbers both show is the power of the internet to bring people together into virtual localities that can develop their own ways with language and practices of translation. These 'local' communities can be observed by anyone, and so can have global repercussions: they are not just local but 'glocal'.

Glocal translation stands in contrast to the official channels with which this chapter began: not standard national languages but community-based, minority, and dialectal tongues; not translation as efficient communication but translation as revealing and relishing differences between languages, and the role of the individual in making sense.

I stumbled across a new website, Transferre, dedicated to translation between dialects and small languages. There is some poetry in Welsh with a Galician translation, both spoken and printed, and an English translation too:

> Cerddoriaeth gynta ein gwlad
> oedd pitran y glaw yn y coed
>
> A primeira música do noso país
> foi o repenique da choiva no bosque
>
> The first music of our country
> was the pitter-patter of rain in the woods.

I don't know Welsh or Galician, but I can still piece together something of what the words mean in those tongues. I can enjoy the brief rain-shower of their music.

Chapter 7
Translational literature

National literatures

The word 'literature' likes to be located. It can be attached to a region of the world—'African Literature', 'South American Literature'—or to a language: 'Arabic Literature', 'Latin Literature'. Most of all, it clings to nation-states, especially European ones: 'French Literature', 'Italian Literature', 'Russian Literature'. One especially complex example is 'English Literature'. A typical 'Eng Lit' course at university will include some English-language writing from Ireland, Scotland, Wales, the United States, India, Africa, Australia, and perhaps elsewhere. But it will present all this diverse material as being related to the culture of the nation of England within the State of the United Kingdom of Great Britain and Northern Ireland.

According to this geography of imaginative writing, any given poem or book or play belongs to 'a literature'. And a literature typically attaches to 'a language' which expresses 'a culture' (often a national culture). Assumptions about translation adhere to this way of thinking. It suggests that the task of the literary translator must be to take a text that belongs in one literature-language-culture and recreate it in another. The emphasis on nationality in literature nourishes the view I have called, 'Translation Rigidly Conceived'.

However, this idea of literature is only a partial construction, one that is historically and geographically contingent. It began to solidify in Europe during the 18th century when the national circulation of books and especially newspapers helped people to feel that they were inhabiting a shared national culture. If you live in Bordeaux and you know you are reading the same news as someone in Paris then you will feel that you belong to the same 'imagined community'. In the UK, publishers produced anthologies with titles like *Moore's British Classics* or *The Works of the English Poets*. In Germany, intellectuals elaborated a philosophy of cultural nationhood. For Johann Wilhelm Gottfried Herder, different literatures were the manifestation of different national spirits (*Volksgeister*).

During the 19th century, liberal nationalists drew on this thinking in their opposition to autocratic regimes. Back then, today's nation-state of Italy was divided between the Austro-Hungarian empire and several smaller kingdoms and dukedoms; but Giuseppe Mazzini and his followers believed it was destined to become united and independent. The reason lay not in economics or geography so much as in literature. As Mazzini's Scottish friend Thomas Carlyle put it: 'poor Italy lies dismembered, scattered asunder, not appearing in any protocol or treaty as a unity at all; yet the noble Italy is actually *one*: Italy produced its Dante; Italy can speak!'.

This use of literature as a nation-building force reappears in many places around the world. In Shanghai in the 1930s, an editor named Zhao Jiabi set about producing a *Compendium of Modern Chinese Literature* ('文学', *wenxue*). He wanted to promote a leftist imagining of a Chinese nation: Western ideas about the role of literature, which had reached him via Japan, offered a way of doing so. In India, during the British Empire, applicants to join the civil service had to take an exam in British literature. As Lord Macaulay, the Victorian architect of this policy, had proclaimed: 'wherever British literature spreads, may it be attended by British virtue and

British freedom!' In the United Kingdom too, Eng Lit courses in school and university were designed with nation-building in mind.

This set of assumptions contributes to the idea that literature is untranslatable. If a literary text crucially belongs to one language-and-nation which is separate from the others then translators are inevitably going to fail the requirements of 'Translation Rigidly Conceived'. They are never going to recreate that text in the medium of another language-and-nation. Those pragmatic kinds of equivalence which—as we have seen—are accepted as translation in many varieties of language-use seem insufficient for literature. What matters in literature—the usual thinking goes—is its intense embeddedness in a particular language and culture. And so the familiar laments rise up: no translation can ever be as good as the original! Poetry is what is lost in translation!

But what if there are other ways of configuring the global geography of imaginative writing? What if literature is not as tied to single languages and national traditions as this one way of thinking, rooted in the West and dominant during the 19th and 20th centuries, made it seem?

Multilingual writing

Samuel Beckett wrote literary texts in both English and French, and translated between the two. Vladimir Nabokov wrote both Russian and American English, and translated between the two. Joseph Conrad had Polish for his first language and French for his second; but he wrote his fiction in English—a mode of English that was enriched and angled by Polish and French, just as Nabokov's American English was energized by his Russian and Beckett's two languages sparked off each other.

Rainer Maria Rilke wrote poems in French as well as German. In fact, French appears in many books that might seem to belong to different literatures. Leo Tolstoy's great Russian novel *War and Peace* incorporates long passages of French, and of Russian that has been Frenchified. Charlotte Brontë's English novel *Villette* includes stretches of French, as does *Tristram Shandy* by Laurence Sterne (along with some Latin). The Irish playwright Oscar Wilde wrote most of his plays in English but chose French for one of them, *Salomé*. William Beckford was an English writer but his novel *Vathek* is in French. Jean Rhys's fictions set in Paris play French and English against each other.

T. S. Eliot sometimes wrote in French, too; and his poem *The Waste Land* also has lines in German, Italian, Latin, and transliterated Sanskrit. Ezra Pound's *Cantos* include several European languages alongside Mandarin Chinese. The strange idiom of James Joyce's *Finnegans Wake* is a compound of many languages. This kind of work is often said to be typical of modernism but in fact multilingual writing has always happened in Europe. Dante Alighieri wrote much Latin and a bit of Provençal as well as Italian. The 'macaronics' of Teofilo Folengo in the 16th century blended Latin with Italian dialects. A century later, John Milton wrote poems in Greek, Latin, and Italian as well as English. And multilingual writing flourishes today, for instance in work by Yoko Tawada (German, Japanese) or Isabel del Rio (Spanish, English).

These examples (and there are many more) challenge the contrast that is sometimes drawn between the national literatures of Europe and the proliferatively multilingual imaginative cultures of India, Africa, and East Asia. Of course it is vital to recognize the plurality of those cultures, where there are forms such as Sanskrit drama in which only the posh characters speak Sanskrit while humbler ones use a different language, Prakrit, and where there are experiences such as that of the Indian writer A. K. Ramanujan: 'in my early years, I spoke Madras Tamil to Amma, I switched to Mysore Tamil with our Iyengar housemaids who cooked for us; outside the house, I spoke Kannada with friends. Upstairs in his office, Appa conversed in English.' When you read the Nigerian novelist Chinua Achebe, it is important to know how his work relates to its multilingual context. He chose English as a language that could span Nigeria as well as reach a global audience, but at the same time he inflected the idiom of the British Empire with his tribal language, Igbo.

However, the contrast between these multilingual cultures on the one hand, and European national literatures on the other, is too simple. As the instances I have mentioned show, European literary culture is multilingual too.

It is true that many European authors chose to stick to one language in their literary writing. But when they did so it was often speckled or shaded with other tongues. Robert Browning's poetry is sometimes peppered with Greek (as in *Aristophanes' Apology*) and it is often designed to sound a bit Italian. Marcel Proust formed his extraordinary style through long study of John Ruskin's English.

And authors who keep to one language for their own writing can also be translators. Chaucer translated from Italian, French, and Latin. Alexander Pope translated Homer. H.D. (Hilda Doolittle) translated Euripides. Cesare Pavese (like many other modern Italian writers) translated much from English and American. Haruki Murakami, the Japanese novelist, and Lydia Davis, the American short-story writer, are both also importantly translators.

Forms and influences traverse languages. Byron adopted the modes of Italian comic romance. Pushkin learned from Byron in French translations by Amédée Pichot and Eusèbe de Salle. Elizabeth Barrett Browning drew on Aeschylus, Dante, Madame de Staël, and George Sand. Henry James was influenced as much by Flaubert and Turgenev (who came to him through French, German, and English translation) as by his Anglophone precursors Nathaniel Hawthorne or George Eliot. Goethe was inspired by the Persian poems of Hafez translated by Joseph von Hammer. Shakespeare drew on Latin, Greek, Italian, and French sources (in translation and sometimes in the original). He grew his style from a language that had recently been massively enriched via translation. Phrases like 'to castigate thy pride' or 'Jove multipotent' bear the marks of this translational energy ('castigate' and 'multipotent' are from the Latin 'castigare' and 'multipotens'). They are like snippets from a chaotic bilingual dictionary.

Even those writers who are most devoted to cultivating a national language pursue that path in the awareness of other possibilities. Wordsworth is one example: he contrasted his style to that of other poets whose diction was closer to Latin. Writing in one language can also reveal the differences between its varieties. This is what happens in Dickens with his brilliant ear for idiom and slang. Oliver Twist (to give just one example) has to learn to translate the inner-city dialect of the Artful Dodger as though it were a foreign tongue.

So Western literature is multilingual too, and always has been. How does this matter to translation?

Translaterature

As we saw in Chapter 2, languages are not separate entities that can be lined up in parallel. The relationship between any one language and any other is always complicated, a mixture of differences, overlaps, and false friends. And languages are themselves internally divided into different dialects, registers, and habits of speech.

It follows—as we saw in Chapters 3 and 4—that translation is not a matter of trying (and of course failing) to achieve sameness with the source text. The meaning and character of the source text are not simply there for the taking: they have to be conjured up, co-created by you as you read. If you then go on to translate, you make a new text, out of different materials, in a different context. You want it to stand in for the source text insofar as that is possible in the changed circumstances: to do a similar job or have a similar effect. But whatever you have written is then of course put into the hands of readers who will interpret it in its turn, each in their own way.

For many kinds of language use, the norms for writing, translation, and interpretation are all strongly regulated. Examples we have looked at include news reports and United Nations resolutions. But literature is an arena of imaginative and linguistic play. Fiction allows anything to happen. Poetic form pushes words together in new ways. Any kind or combination of language can appear on a literary page. Translation in the loose sense—translationality, as I've called it—is fundamental to literary writing: words are carried over into new contexts, ideas are rephrased in surprising ways. Translation across languages joins in these processes. The stimulus of another language can prompt a fresh way of seeing, and saying. A different culture can offer new narrative possibilities and other modes of being.

This inherent translationality of literary writing creates particular difficulties but also particular opportunities for the literary translator. Let's look at an example. Alexander Pope's *The Rape of the Lock* was published in successive, ever-growing editions between 1712 and 1717. It recounts a scandalous episode in high society: an unnamed Baron snips a lock of hair from the beauteous head of Belinda, an it-girl of the time. The story is told in mock-heroic style: that is to say, it uses the language of epic poetry to make fun of this tea-cup tempest. Narrative episodes and turns of phrase are translationally brought onto the page from Homer's *Iliad*, which Pope himself would translate in the coming years, and Virgil's *Aeneid*, which had been brilliantly and famously translated by John Dryden two decades before.

At one point, the Baron prays to the gods to let him both snip the lock and keep it:

> The Pow'rs gave Ear, and granted half his Pray'r,
> The rest, the winds dispers'd in empty Air.

Pope's lines replay a famous episode from the *Aeneid* where one of Aeneas's allies, Arruns, prays to defeat the Volscian warrior Camilla and to survive to return home. Dryden had translated the moment like this:

> *Apollo* heard, and granting half his Pray'r
> Shuffled in Winds the rest, and toss'd in empty Air.

Pope takes a lot from Dryden, as alert readers would have been aware. But he also makes some changes that move his English closer to Virgil's Latin:

> Audiit et voti Phoebus succedere partem
> Mente dedit, partem volucris dispersit in auras.

Dryden had opted to mark his difference from Virgil with energetic words that had their roots in old English: 'shuffled', 'toss'd'. But Pope's phrase 'dispers'd in . . . air' blends expressively into the Latin *dispersit in auras*.

The effect of Pope's lines comes from their involvement in a translational nexus. It is as though they are saying: 'look how close we are to this tragic moment in Virgil (even closer than Dryden was!)'—while at the same time making the Baron's prayer seem utterly trivial in comparison. The poetry's translationality creates a complex, particular nuance: it is the sort of thing that makes people despair of the translation of literature in the model of 'Translation Rigidly Conceived'.

However, these lines' translationality also creates an opportunity, as a recent Italian translation by Viola Papetti reveals:

> i numi ascoltarono, e per metà esaudirono la prece,
> il resto, i venti lo dispersero per l'aere vuoto.

The closeness of Pope's words to Latin means that they are also close to Italian. *Dispersero per l'aere* has overlaps of sound as well as meaning with 'dispersed in ... air' and establishes a similar relationship with the Virgil. The contrast with Dryden has dropped away, of course, since that was a function of Pope's location in England in the early 18th century. But a different literary connection has sprung up in its place. The phrase *per l'aere* plus an adjective was used often by Dante in the *Divine Comedy*: *per l'aere nero, per l'aere perso, per l'aere maligno*, and so on ('through the black air', 'the dark air', 'the malignant air'). And Dante, just like Dryden, was a poet much indebted to Virgil.

There are, then, gains as well as losses in this act of translation. What is lost is the particular expressive triangulation of Pope's line, as well as its rhythm and rhyme. But a different triangulation is gained, together with a new awareness of the breadth of the multilingual, post-epic tradition in which Pope was writing. The Italian translation shows that aspects of Virgil that inspired Pope also mattered to Dante. It reveals an unexpected kinship between two quite different writers who never read each other's work.

There is a famous essay by the early 20th-century German intellectual Walter Benjamin, 'Die Aufgabe des Übersetzers' ('The Task of the Translator'). What's attractive about it is the richness of the language it uses for making sense of translation. Instead of the usual talk of accuracy or equivalence, Benjamin speaks of translation as 'survival' (*Überleben*), unfolding (*Entfaltung*), and 'after-ripening' (*Nachreife*). These words express the feeling that a literary text is not just a block of print on a page or screen but rather a wellspring of imaginative potential which plays out when the text is read, responded to, reinterpreted, and translated.

Papetti's Italian *The Rape of the Lock* is a small instance of what Benjamin had in mind. It is not a particularly distinguished translation: in the lines we have looked at, it is the overlap of languages, more than the individual translator, that has created the ripening effect. In really brilliant translations, the energies of the languages involved combine with the genius of the translator to create distinctive modes of expression. I call this 'the poetry of translation'.

One instance is *Cathay*, Ezra Pound's collection of poem-translations from ancient Chinese. As we saw in Chapter 1, Pound models his English on the sequence of the Chinese characters, creating a style which strangely combines reticence and emotion. A note at the start of the book explains the distance the imaginative impulse of the writing has had to travel in order to reach its place and year of publication, London, 1915: 'For the most part from the Chinese of Rihaku (Li T'ai Po), from the notes of the late Ernest Fenollosa, and the decipherings of the professors Mori and Ariga.'

So when readers turn to the first poem-translation in *Cathay*, 'Song of the Bowmen of Shu', they are aware that the words emerge from a combination of places, from ancient China and an England at war:

> Here we are, picking the first fern-shoots
> And saying: 'When shall we get back to our country?'
> Here we are because we have the Ken-in for our foemen,
> We have no comfort because of these Mongols.

The words point to the Western Front as much as to the ancient conflict involving 'the Ken-in' whose identity is likely to be obscure to most English readers. The imaginative charge of the writing comes from the way it links modern warfare to unknown battles far away and long ago. It is translation that brings this connection into being.

The poetry of translation can conjure all sorts of imaginative relationships. It can explore desire, as in Dryden's translation from Lucretius, 'Concerning the Nature of Love'; and loss, as in Anne Carson's *Nox*, from Catullus's elegiac poem no. 101; and many forms of change, as in Edward FitzGerald's *Rubáiyát of Omar Khayyám*. It can layer languages, times, places, and people, and trace the continuities and disparities between them.

Prose writing too can grow in translation. W. G. Sebald lived in East Anglia but wrote in German: his books, which mingle fiction and autobiography, explore displacement, memory, and loss. In the English translations by Michael Hulse and Anthea Bell, Sebald's books have enjoyed great success. Part of the reason must lie in the harmony between the slightly dislocated feel of the translated writing and Sebald's thematic concerns. Here is the beginning of *Austerlitz*, translated by Bell:

> In the second half of the 1960s I travelled repeatedly from England to Belgium, partly for study purposes, partly for other reasons which were never entirely clear to me, staying sometimes for just one or two days, sometimes for several weeks.

The style has a precision which feels slightly strange while at the same time suggesting great care in the choice of words. It is in English but perhaps not completely of it, in the same way as the speaker is not wholly settled in England. The effect is (of course) a bit different from the German, but not in a way that feels like loss. Here, just as with Pound's *Cathay*, the layered language of translation has an aptness to the imaginative endeavour of the writing. This precise, displaced, questioning voice probes the unknowable both here in the opening sentence ('reasons which were never entirely clear to me') and throughout the book.

It is sometimes said that translation poses a danger to literature. In our globalized world—the argument goes—we will get used to reading in translation, and authors will learn to write in a way that makes it easier for their work to be translated. And since translation—the assumption is—can never be as stylistically alive as original writing, the result will be a gradual deadening of linguistic and imaginative possibility.

Certainly translations are often flatter than their source texts. Sometimes the translator is not that good a stylist; sometimes the linguistic challenges of translation are too great. But there is also a literature of translation—shall we call it 'translaterature'?—made up of works which grow as they are translated, developing new complexity and power.

The theatre of translation

The theatre is an inherently translational form. On the one hand, each performance is vividly present. It is done by human beings in front of other human beings, all of them experiencing the work together for the same short stretch of time. It is, as we say, 'live'. On the other hand, each performance is also a repeat. It carries over materials and meanings from earlier performances. Because it is live, something will inevitably be slightly different each time: attending a second performance is different from re-watching a video. Even the first night of a new play repeats the previews which repeat the rehearsals, each reiteration departing slightly from the last. A performance of a great classic will repeat and differ from many other performances and productions in other places, times, and languages.

Translation for the theatre becomes part of this fluid practice of reiteration and change. The bones of a great drama can be re-articulated in many ways. The story of Phaedra, who loved her husband's son Hippolytus with tragic consequences, was staged in ancient Athens by Euripides with the title *Hippolytus*. It was reworked in Latin by Seneca the Younger as *Phaedra*, in French by Jean Racine as *Phèdre* (1677), in Italian by Gabriele D'Annunzio as *Fedra* (1909), in Spanish by Miguel de Unamuno as *Fedra* (1911), in American English by Eugene O'Neill as *Desire under the Elms* (1924), in Russian by Marina Tsvetaeva as *Fedra* (1928), in English by Tony Harrison as *Phaedra Britannica* (1975), in Swedish by Per Olov Enquist as *Till Fedra* (1980), in English again by Sarah Kane as *Phaedra's Love* (1996)—to mention but a few of the many re-workings and fresh productions in these and other languages. The same goes for many other classic dramas.

These theatrical modes of recreation mingle translation, adaptation, and re-writing, and blend them with new production ideas and acting styles: the term 'tradaptation' is sometimes used. The overriding aim is to make the play work in the moment of performance. In a tradaptation of Macbeth, Zulu playwright Welcome Msomi dropped the famous image of the milk of human kindness as being unlikely to play well in the Zulu context. Instead, his stand-in for Lady Macbeth fears the dove in her husband's heart.

Closer translations too need above all to use speakable words. In Peter Carson's Penguin Classics translation of Chekhov's *Ivanov*, a character at one point says: 'It's so frightfully boring that I'd simply like to run off and bang my head on a wall. And Lord have mercy on us all!' In a version by David Harrower for the National Theatre in London in 2002 this became 'I'm so bored I want to take a run at a wall.' Here, as often in translational work for the theatre, the English words came into being through the work of at least two people: a translator to engage with the source text and a playwright to adapt it for an audience.

Translation for the theatre, then, is a specially stark instance of the truth that we explored in Chapters 3 and 4. Translation is never simply into 'a language', but always into a kind of language, in a situation, for a purpose. Even the size of the performance space can make a difference. Andrea Peghinelli translated Philip Ridley's 1991 play *The Pitchfork Disney* into Italian. The version for an open-air production in Spoleto had to be altered when the show transferred to a small fringe theatre in Rome: 'It's really different when you pronounce a line and you have to walk for seven or eight metres or if you just have to take two or three steps...some of the extensive monologues would have not been "tolerated" by the different audience in that claustrophobic auditorium.'

Since theatre is so immediate, productions often take on contemporary relevance. Shakespeare's *Measure for Measure*, performed in Russian in Moscow in 2015, became a critique of abuses of power by Vladimir Putin's régime. A South African tradaptation of *Julius Caesar*, *SeZaR*, seemed to comment on a recent assassination when it was performed in Grahamstown in 2001. This can happen with any play, of course, but translation can connect contemporary realities to imaginative materials from far away: it is the same sort of thing as we saw with Pound's *Cathay*. Playwright Colin Teevan found this with *Iph*, his 1999 tradaptation of Euripides's *Iphigenia in Aulis*, which shows a girl being sacrificed for a war effort: 'It was written for Irish voices, but when we did a reading in the Cottesloe [London]...just after the first female suicide bombers in Palestine, people were very affected by that resonance.'

Relevance and speakability are not the only routes to success in theatre translation. The choreography of actors' bodies and voices is tremendously important: language collaborates with expressive movement and sound.

A vivid instance occurred when the Italian dramatic comedian Dario Fo was touring the United States in 1986. He performed in

Italian, with an intepreter, Ron Jenkins, standing beside him and re-speaking his words in English, live. Rhythm and movement were crucial:

> Fo describes an airport arrival of Pope John Paul II. He sets the scene as if it were being depicted in a documentary newscast...until the montage climaxes with the appearance of the pontiff at the door of the aircraft. The pace of Fo's speech builds slowly into a staccato delivery of the details of the pope's appearance. 'Silver hair. Blue eyes. Big smile. Neck of a bull. Pectoral muscles bulging. Abdominal muscles prominent. A belt around his waist. And above all a red cloak down to his feet. SUPERMAN!'

> I discovered through trial and error that the 'Superman' punch line doesn't get a laugh unless the phrases that precede it are short and punchy...The sequential rhythm of the two languages is essential, and Fo uses the beats of my translation to punctuate his description with gestures that pantomime the traits being recalled. *Capelli d'argento*. 'Silver hair'. *Occhi cerulli*. 'Blue eyes'. *Grande sorriso*. 'Big smile'. Italian. English. Italian. English...ba ba da boom...'Superman!'...The anticipation and bravado need to be translated along with the meaning of the words.

The expressive power of body and voice can compel theatre audiences to swallow, and enjoy, peculiar linguistic experiences.

The plays of Samuel Beckett are a good example. Their gestures are precisely choreographed and their words are acutely speakable, but the significance of what is going on is hard to state. Audiences are held fascinated by something strange. Translation helped to bring this effect into being. Beckett sometimes wrote in French and then translated into English, sometimes the other way round. Whatever the direction, the texts in both the languages inhabit a translational imaginative space: either they have come from the other language or they are about to go into it. Literary critic Arnold Kettle didn't like the result. He said the first London production of Beckett's *Waiting for Godot* 'sounds like a bad translation from his own French'. This is unfair to the spark of the play's language, but it also points to something true. Beckett's writing is dramatically alive while also being at a slight angle to the norms of both English and French speech. It's a bit like what we found in the Anthea Bell translation of W. G. Sebald.

Theatre audiences also manage to enjoy performances in foreign languages. It helps if they know the play already in their own tongue, and surtitles are also useful, as they are in opera. Both the 2015 Russian *Measure for Measure* and the 2001 *SeZaR*, which mixed Shakespeare's English with isiZulu, isiXhosa, SeSotho, Tswana, and TsotsiTaal, had successful runs in Britain. This can look like a modern phenomenon, a by-product of globalization: in 2012, London's Globe Theatre staged productions of Shakespeare in thirty-seven languages to coincide with the Olympic Games. In fact, Victorian Londoners, too, happily went along to French and Italian performances of Shakespeare. They felt that the passionate foreigners could reveal depths in the plays which primmer English performances locked down.

On the face of it this is a strange use of translation: to choose to go to a play that has been translated from your own language into a tongue that you cannot understand. But with this sort of performance you pay more attention to movement, gesture, and intonation, bringing all your interpretive powers to bear on the significance of physicality and sound. It can feel like a more intense experience.

All theatre translation relies on the collaborating presence of body language. In this, it differs from other sorts of translation. Of course video subtitling and dubbing are layered on top of the work of actors, but the actors do not adapt their performances to the translation. And translators of fiction or poetry might sometimes read out their work, perhaps in tandem with the source-text author; but a reading is not so rich in added meaning as a theatre production. So the element of performance is a crucial and distinctive aspect of translation for the theatre.

Nevertheless, the special case of the theatre can help throw light on the workings of all translation. Like a theatre production, every translation interprets its source text. You can go to a translation (just as you go to the theatre) to discover new aspects of a work you have already read or seen. This is why, if you are really interested in a text in one language (even your own first language) you should always look at its translations into other languages that you know. The shortcoming of being monolingual is not only that writing in other languages is shut off from you, but also that you lack this resource for increasing your appreciation of writing in your own.

From another point of view, a production is not an interpretation. Rather, it is itself 'the play' which the script has helped bring into being. As we saw in Chapter 4, translations are not just interpretations of their source texts either. They are also new works of imagining that need interpreting in their turn. In many fields, this creative work of translation is both restricted and ignored. Translations of instruction manuals, news articles, United Nations resolutions, and other functional uses of language do always bring something new. But the rules by which these translations are done restrain their creativity as much as possible, and the conventions with which they are interpreted prevent it from being noticed.

But in literature, both in the theatre and in print, the double nature of translation is allowed to flourish. Translations can be seen to be both interpretations of other works and works in themselves. This is how they connect the present to the past, and the here to the elsewhere; how they bridge cultures and the people who inhabit them, allowing contrasts and continuities of ideas, feelings, and instincts to be explored. This is why literary translation is so revealing of what is at stake in translation in general; and also why translational literature is such a powerful imaginative vein.

Two futures

In one future, machine translation is used more and more as an efficient tool. People will no longer feel the need to learn foreign languages intimately. When not relying on their computers, they will be able to communicate with pretty much anyone in global English, a jargon which lacks richness and nuance because it belongs everywhere and nowhere: it is a universal translationese. National languages, no longer needed in the global arenas of business, politics, science, and education, will be used for lesser and lesser purposes. Like so many dialects they will shrivel. They will become the objects of nostalgia and the work of preservation societies. The powers of expression developed over centuries by different languages in different print cultures will stiffen and fade.

In the second future, the internet, migration, and other forces of globalization will make people more aware of linguistic difference. We will use our machine translation programs not just to communicate but to explore different possibilities of expression. As English spreads so will it fracture, with regional and virtual speech communities all shaping it to their own purposes, splitting it as happened once to Latin. Competing global languages such as Mandarin Chinese, Portuguese, and Swahili will not drop away. People will revel in multilingualism, using different languages for different purposes and moods: chatting in one, writing in another, doing business in another again.

Probably neither of these futures will exactly happen. But something of both will come to pass. Each tendency feeds off the other. Translation is in some respects the enemy of languages, a flattening and homogenizing power. But translation is also the lover of languages: it discerns and values difference, and spurs linguistic innovation. Likewise, the point of language itself is not just for us to be able to communicate. It is also to enable us to be different from one another. Languages let us belong to this group rather than that one, be understood by some people more than others—that is to be ourselves.

This is why translation needs to be at the heart of the way we use and think about language. It reveals and relishes difference while also bridging it. It recognizes that Babel was as much a blessing as a curse.

References

Chapter 1: Crossing languages

Nabokov takes this view in his translation and commentary of Alexandr Pushkin, *Eugene Onegin: A Novel in Verse*, 2 vols, rev. edn (Princeton, NJ: Princeton University Press, 1975).

Kanbun-kundoku is described in Judy Wakabayashi, 'The Reconceptualization of Translation from Chinese in 18th-Century Japan', in Eva Hung (ed.), *Translation and Cultural Change: Studies in History, Norms, and Image Projection* (Amsterdam: John Benjamins, 2005), 121–45; see also James Hadley, 'Theorizing in Unfamiliar Contexts: New Directions in Translation Studies' (unpublished PhD thesis: University of East Anglia, 2013).

Ezra Pound, 'The Beautiful Toilet', 1–2, quoted from his *Collected Shorter Poems* (London: Faber and Faber, 1968).

Bernard Lewis, *From Babel to Dragomans: Interpreting the Middle East* (London: Weidenfeld and Nicolson, 2004), 29.

Martha P. Y. Cheung (ed.) *An Anthology of Chinese Discourse on Translation*, vol. 1: *From the Earliest Times to the Buddhist Project* (Manchester: St Jerome, 2006), 7–12.

Ovid's Epistles, translated by several hands (London: Jacob Tonson, 1680).

Chapter 2: Definitions

Martha Cheung (ed.), *An Anthology of Chinese Discourse on Translation*, vol. 1, 7–12.

Maria Tymoczko, *Enlarging Translation, Empowering Translators* (Manchester: St Jerome, 2007), 71.

Ronit Ricci, 'On the Untranslatability of 'Translation': Considerations from Java, Indonesia', in Ronit Ricci and Jan van der Putten (eds), *Translation in Asia: Theories, Practices, Histories* (Manchester: St Jerome, 2011), 58.

The uses of 'to translate' by Lyly, Shakespeare, and others are discussed in Matthew Reynolds, *The Poetry of Translation: From Chaucer & Petrarch to Homer & Logue* (Oxford: OUP, 2011), 1–8.

John Dryden, *The Poems*, ed. Paul Hammond and David Hopkins, 5 vols (London: Longman, 1995–2005), i, 384–5, and iv, 446; John Dryden, *The Works*, ed. E. N. Hooker, H. T. Swedenberg, Jr, et al., 20 vols (Berkeley and London: University of California Press, 1956–2000), v, 329–30. See Reynolds, *The Poetry of Translation*, 73–4.

Derrida's 'Des tours de Babel' appears with a translation by Joseph F. Graham in Joseph F. Graham (ed.), *Difference in Translation* (Ithaca, NY: Cornell University Press, 1985), 165–207 and 209–48.

Myriam Salama-Carr, 'Interpreters in Conflict—The View from Within: An Interview with Louise Askew', *Translation Studies* 4.1 (2011), 103–8, 106.

William Barnes, *Poems of Rural Life in the Dorset Dialect: With a Dissertation and Glossary* (London: John Russell Smith, 1844), 11–12; Dryden, *Poems* v, 80.

George Steiner, *After Babel: Aspects of Language and Translation* (1975; 3rd edn, Oxford: OUP, 1998), xii, 49. The discussion here draws on my argument in *The Poetry of Translation*, 9–11.

Chapter 3: Words, contexts, and purposes

Christine Brooke-Rose, *Between* (1968), in *The Brooke-Rose Omnibus* (Manchester: Carcanet, 1986), 417–18.

J. C. Catford, *A Linguistic Theory of Translation* (Oxford: OUP, 1965), 49.

The French predilection for nouns is detailed in J. P. Vinay and J. Darbelnet, *Stylistique comparée du Français et de l'Anglais* (Paris: Didier, 1973), 103.

The instructions for a Morris dance are from 'Jigs—An Aide Memoire' at <http://www.themorrisring.org/sides/jigs-some-thoughts>, accessed 25 September 2015.

Catford, *A Linguistic Theory of Translation*, 39.

Tony Harrison, *Theatre Works 1973–1985* (Harmondsworth: Penguin, 1986), 190.

Aeschylus, *Oresteia*, tr. Alan H. Sommerstein (Cambridge, MA, and London: Harvard University Press, 2005), 5.

Robert Browning, *Poetical Works*, 16 vols (London: Smith, Elder & Co, 1888–89), xiii, 269.

Chapter 4: Forms, identities, and interpretations

The International Language of ISO Graphical Symbols (Geneva: ISO Central Secretariat, 2013), 15, 18, 22.

Gordon Brotherston, *Image of the New World: The American Continent Portrayed in Native Texts* (London: Thames and Hudson, 1979), 51–2.

The example of the Chinese sentence is from Mona Baker, *In Other Words: A Coursebook on Translation*, 2nd edn (Abingdon: Routledge, 2011), 154.

Dante Alighieri, *Hell*, tr. Dorothy L. Sayers (Harmondsworth: Penguin, 1949), 1.

Dante Alighieri, *The Divine Comedy*, tr. Henry Wadsworth Longfellow, 3 vols (London: George Routledge and Sons, 1867), i, 1.

Friedrich Schleiermacher, 'Ueber die verschiedenen Methoden des Uebersezens', in Hans Joachim Störig (ed.), *Das Problem des Übersetzens* (Darmstadt: Wissenschaftliche Buchgesellschaft, 1963), 47.

The binary of foreignizing and domesticating was given prominence by Lawrence Venuti in *The Translator's Invisibility: A History of Translation* (Abingdon: Routledge, 1995; 2nd edn, 2008).

Interpretation in the Asylum Process: Guide for Interpreters (Helsinki: Finnish Immigration Service Refugee Advice Centre, 2010), 9. <http://www.migri.fi/download/16471_Tulkkaus_ turvapaikkamenettelyssa_Opas_tulkeille_en.pdf?fd6e5908f746d288>, accessed 27 May 2015.

Andrew Bank, *Bushmen in a Victorian World: The Remarkable Story of the Bleek-Lloyd Collection of Bushman Folklore* (Cape Town: Double Storey, 2006), 87.

Specimens of Bushman Folklore, collected by the late W. H. I. Bleek, PhD, and L. C. Lloyd, edited by the latter, with an introduction by George McCall Theal (London: George Allen and Company, 1911), 84–5.

Dan Gunn's review was in *The Times Literary Supplement* 5466 (4 January 2008), 23; the Bassani and the Weaver translation are

quoted in McKendrick's reply, *The Times Literary Supplement*
5472 (15 February 2008), 6.

The *Consolidated Version of the Treaty on European Union* is quoted
from <http://eur-lex.europa.eu/legal-content/en/
TXT/?uri=CELEX:12012M/TXT>, accessed 10 June 2015.

Chapter 5: Power, religion, and choice

Polybius, *Histories* 20. 9–10; the consul's reply is given in Livy, *Ab urbe
condita* 36.28. Both texts are quoted from the *Perseus Digital
Library*: <http://www.perseus.tufts.edu/hopper/>, accessed
2 June 2015. See Michael Cronin, *Translation in the Digital Age*
(Abingdon: Routledge, 2013), 15.

Humpty Dumpty is in Lewis Carroll, *Alice's Adventures in
Wonderland and Through the Looking Glass*, ed. Hugh Haughton
(Harmondsworth: Penguin, 1998), 186.

United Nations Security Council Resolution 242 is discussed in
Bernard Lewis, *From Babel to Dragomans: Interpreting the Middle
East* (London: Weidenfeld and Nicolson, 2004), 30.

Texts of the Treaty of Waitangi, with commentary, are at <http://
www.nzhistory.net.nz/politics/treaty-of-waitangi>, accessed
25 September 2015. The historical context is discussed in
Sabine Fenton and Paul Moon, 'The Translation of the Treaty of
Waitangi: A Case of Disempowerment', in Maria Tymoczko
and Edwin Gentzler (eds), *Translation and Power* (Amherst:
University of Massachusetts Press, 2002), 25–44: Lord
Normanby is quoted on p. 30 and Kaitaia Chief Napera
Panakareao on p. 40.

The American evangelical website is <https://www.wycliffe.org/about/
why>, accessed 10 June 2015.

Haslina Haroun, 'Early Discourse on Translation in Malay: The Views
of Abdullah bin Abdul Kadir Munsyi', in Ronit Ricci and Jan van
der Putten (eds), *Translation in Asia: Theories, Practices, Histories*
(Manchester: St Jerome, 2011), 73–87, 76.

Eugene Nida, *Toward a Science of Translating: With Special Reference
to Principles and Procedures Involved in Bible Translating*
(Leiden: E. J. Brill, 1964), 160.

William A Smalley, *Translation as Mission: Bible Translation in
the Modern Missionary Movement* (Macon, GA: Mercer, 1991),
3, 41, 174.

Jost Oliver Zetzsche, *The Bible in China: The History of the Union Version or The Culmination of Protestant Missionary Bible Translation in China* (Nettetal, GE: Sankt Augustin, 1999), 77–82.

A. C. Partridge, *English Biblical Translation* (London: Deutsch, 1973), 22, 41, 95.

Luther is quoted in Daniel Weissbort and Astradur Eysteinsson (eds), *Translation—Theory and Practice: A Historical Reader* (Oxford: OUP, 2006), 57–62.

Aquinas's translation is quoted in Joseph A. Fitzmyer, *Romans, A New Translation with Introduction and Commentary* (New York: Doubleday, 1993), 360–1.

Travis Zadeh, *The Vernacular Qur'an: Translation and the Rise of Persian Exegesis* (London: OUP, in association with the Institute of Ismaili Studies, 2012), 1–19.

A recent instance of parallel text is *Al-Qur'ān: A Contemporary Translation*, tr. Ahmed Ali, revised printing (Princeton, NJ: Princeton University Press, 2001).

Kate Sturge, 'Censorship of Translated Fiction in Nazi Germany', *TTR: traductions, terminologie, rédaction* 15.2 (2002), 153–69.

Marta Rioja Barrocal, 'English-Spanish Translations and Censorship in Spain 1962–1969', *inTRAlinea* 12 (2010): <http://www.intralinea.org/archive/article/1658>, accessed 7 June 2015.

Camino Gutiérrez Lanza, 'Spanish Film Translation and Cultural Patronage: The Filtering and Manipulation of Imported Material during Franco's Dictatorship', in Maria Tymoczko and Edwin Gentzler (eds), *Translation and Power* (Amherst: University of Massachusetts Press, 2002), 141–59, 147.

Guido Bonsaver, 'Fascist Censorship on Literature and the Case of Elio Vittorini', *Modern Italy* 8.2 (2003), 165–86, 175.

Matthew Reynolds, 'Semi-Censorship in Browning and Dryden', in Francesca Billiani (ed.), *Modes of Censorship and Translation: National Contexts and Diverse Media* (Manchester: St Jerome, 2007), 187–204.

Matthew Reynolds, *Likenesses: Translation, Illustration, Interpretation* (Oxford: Legenda, 2013), 89.

Irish Translators' and Interpreters' Association Cumann Aistritheoirí Agus Teangairí na Héireann Code of Practice and Professional Ethics, Articles 5.1.3 and 4.1: <http://translatorsassociation.ie/component/option,com_docman/task,cat_view/gid,21/Itemid,61/>; see Julie McDonough Dolmaya, 'Moral Ambiguity: Some

Shortcomings of Professional Codes of Ethics for Translators', *The Journal of Specialised Translation* 15 (2011): <http://www.jostrans.org/issue15/art_mcdonough.php>, accessed 22 July 2015.

Primo Levi, *Se questo è un uomo* (1947; Milan: Einaudi, 1958), 21. See Michael Cronin *Translation and Identity* (Abingdon: Routledge, 2006), 77.

Gayatri Chakravorty Spivak, *Outside in the Teaching Machine* (Abingdon: Routledge, 1993), 183.

Meena T. Pillai, 'Gendering Translation, Translating Gender', in N. Kamala (ed.), *Translating Women: Indian Interventions* (New Delhi: Zubaan, 2009), 1–15, 13.

Gloucestershire County Council, 'Interpretation and Translation: Policy and Guidance for Staff': <http://www.gloucestershire.gov.uk/extra/CHttpHandler.ashx?id=49179&p=0>, accessed 30 June 2016.

'Trials collapsing thanks to "shambolic" privatisation of translation services': <http://www.theguardian.com/law/2013/feb/06/court-interpreting-services-privatisation-shambolic>, accessed 12 July 2015.

Rabia Rehmen, 'Translator', in Kate Clanchy (ed.), *The Path: An Anthology by the First Story Group at Oxford Spires Academy* (London: First Story Limited, 2015), 20.

Annalisa Sandrelli, 'Gli interpreti presso il tribunale penale di Roma: Un'indagine empirica', *inTRAlinea*, 12 July 2015, 13: <http://www.intralinea.org/archive/article/1670>, accessed 15 July 2015.

William J. Spurlin, 'Queering Translation', in Sandra Bermann and Catherine Porter (eds), *A Companion to Translation Studies* (Chichester: Wiley-Blackwell, 2014), 298–309, 300, 307.

Antoine Berman, *l'Épreuve de l'étranger: culture et traduction dans l'Allemagne romantique: Herder, Goethe, Schlegel, Novalis, Humboldt, Schleiermacher, Hölderlin* (Paris: Gallimard, 1984).

Chapter 6: Words in the world

The Index Translationum is at <http://portal.unesco.org/culture/en/ev.php-URL_ID=7810&URL_DO=DO_TOPIC&URL_SECTION=201.html>.

Information about translation in the European Parliament is at <http://www.europarl.europa.eu/aboutparliament/en/20150201PVL00013/Multilingualism>, accessed 25 July 2015.

The hours of debate in each language are from <http://www.theguardian.com/education/datablog/2014/may/21/european-parliament-english-language-official-debates-data>, accessed 25 July 2015.

Deborah Cao and Xingmin Zhao, 'Translation at the United Nations as Specialized Translation', *Journal of Specialised Translation* 9 (2008), 39–54, 48–51.

Esperança Bielsa and Susan Bassnett, *Translation in Global News* (Abingdon: Routledge, 2009), 57, 108–10, 63.

Karen Stetting, 'Transediting: A New Term for Coping with the Grey Area between Editing and Translating', in Graham Caie, Kirsten Haastrup, Arnt Lykke Jakobsen, et al. (eds), *Proceedings from the Fourth Nordic Conference for English Studies* (Copenhagen: University of Copenhagen, 1989), 371–82.

The example of machine translation from Russian is quoted from F. Knowles, 'Error Analysis of Systran Output—a suggested criterion for the internal evaluation of translation quality and a possible corrective for system design', in Barbara M. Snell (ed.), *Translating and the Computer* (Amsterdam and Oxford: North-Holland, 1979), 109–33, 130, quoted in David Crystal, *The Cambridge Encyclopedia of Language*, 2nd edn (Cambridge: CUP, 1997), 352.

<http://www.tripadvisor.co.uk/Hotel_Review-g297409-d455433-Reviews-Jinjiang_Sunshine_Hotel-Lanzhou_Gansu.html>, accessed 25 July 2015.

Information about the needs of multinationals is from <http://www.sdl.com/about>, accessed 23 July 2015.

Global Voices: <http://globalvoicesonline.org/about/>, accessed 15 July 2015.

Mosireen: <http://mosireen.org/>, accessed 15 July 2015.

Wikipedia's instructions for translation: <https://en.wikipedia.org/wiki/Wikipedia:WikiProject_Echo>, accessed 28 July 2015.

TED's instructions for subtitling: <https://www.ted.com/participate/translate/guidelines>, accessed 28 July 2015.

Words of Women from the Egyptian Revolution are at <https://www.facebook.com/HerstoryEgypt>; see the discussion by Mona Baker at <http://www.monabaker.org/?p=1567>, accessed 26 September 2015.

A description, by Ahmed Refaat, of the Cairo conference organized by Mona Baker, Yasmin El Rifae, and Mada Masr is at <http://www.monabaker.org/?p=1129>, accessed 30 June 2016.

Ifor ap Glyn, 'glaw', lines 1–2, translated by David Miranda-Barreiro and Philip R. Davies, *Transferre*: <https://valentinagosetti.wordpress.com/2015/06/23/welsh-poetry-into-galician-ifor-ap-glyn-translated-by-david-miranda-barreiro-and-philip-r-davies/>, accessed 4 July 2015.

Chapter 7: Translational literature

Benedict Anderson, *Imagined Communities: Reflections on the Origin and Spread of Nationalism* (London: Verso, 1983).

Herder, *Briefe zu Beförderung der Humanität*, 1797, in his *Sämmtliche Werke*, 33 vols, ed. Bernhard Suphan et al. (Berlin: Weidmann, 1883), xviii, 134–40.

Thomas Carlyle, *On Heroes, Hero-Worship and the Heroic in History* (1840; London: Chapman and Hall, 1897), 114; see Matthew Reynolds, *The Realms of Verse, 1830–1870: English Poetry in a Time of Nation-Building* (Oxford: OUP, 2001), 17.

Lydia H. Liu, *Translingual Practice: Literature, National Culture and Translated Modernity: China, 1900–1937* (Stanford, CA: Stanford University Press, 1995), 214–17.

Macaulay is quoted in Chris Baldick, *The Social Mission of English Criticism, 1848–1932* (Oxford: Clarendon Press, 1987), 70.

Ramanujan is quoted by Naita Gokhale, 'Negotiating Multilingual Literary Spaces': <http://www.india-seminar.com/2009/600/600_namita_gokhale.htm>, accessed 12 September 2105.

William Shakespeare, *Timon of Athens*, IV. iii. 241 and *Troilus and Cressida* IV. vii. 13.

Alexander Pope, *The Rape of the Lock*, 2. 45–46, tr. as *Il Riccio Rapito* by Viola Papetti (Milan: Rizzoli, 1984), 64.

John Dryden, *The Aeneis of Vergil*, 11. 794–5; Virgil, *Aeneid*, 11. 794–5.

Walter Benjamin, *Illuminationen. Ausgewählte Schriften*, vol. 1 (Frankfurt am Main: Suhrkamp, 1977), 50–9.

Ezra Pound, 'Song of the Bowmen of Shu', 1–4, quoted from his *Collected Shorter Poems* (London: Faber and Faber, 1968).

W. G. Sebald, *Austerlitz*, tr. Anthea Bell (London: Penguin, 2001), 1.

One version of the argument that translation poses a danger to literature is made by Tim Parks, 'Literature without Style', *NYR Daily*, <http://www.nybooks.com/blogs/nyrblog/2013/nov/07/literature-without-style/>, accessed 26 September 2015.

Martin Orkin, '"I am the tusk of an elephant"—Macbeth, Titus and Caesar in Johannesburg', in A. J. Hoenselaars (ed.), *Shakespeare and the Language of Translation* (London: Arden, 2004), 270–88.

The Chekhov example is from Brian Logan 'Whose Play is it Anyway?', *The Guardian*, 12 March 2003: <http://www.theguardian.com/stage/2003/mar/12/theatre.artsfeatures>, accessed 10 September 2015.

Andrea Peghinelli, 'Theatre Translation as Collaboration: A Case in Point in British Contemporary Drama', *Journal for Communication and Culture* 2.1 (2012), 20–30, 26.

Russian reviews of the 2015 Moscow *Measure for Measure* are quoted at <http://www.cheekbyjowl.com/measure_for_measure.php>, accessed 11 September 2015.

Laurence Wright, 'Confronting the African Nightmare: Yael Farber's *SeZaR*', *Shakespeare in Southern Africa* 13 (2001): 102–4.

Colin Teevan was speaking at a roundtable 'On Translation' chaired by Christopher Campbell, Olivier Theatre, London, 11 November 2003: <http://www.nationaltheatre.org.uk/discover-more/platforms/platform-papers/on-translation>, accessed 11th September 2015; information no longer on website.

Ron Jenkins, 'The Rhythms of Resurrection', in Joseph Farrell and Antonio Scude (eds), *Dario Fo: Stage, Text, and Tradition* (Carbondale, IL: Southern Illinois University Press, 2000), 29–38, 34.

Arnold Kettle is quoted in Sinéad Mooney, *A Tongue not Mine: Beckett and Translation* (Oxford: OUP, 2011), 178.

Victorians watching foreign-language Shakespeare are discussed in Matthew Reynolds, 'Theatrical Allusion', *Essays in Criticism*, 55.1 (2005), 80–8.

Further reading

Chapter 1: Crossing languages

Paul Hammond, *Dryden and the Traces of Classical Rome* (Oxford: OUP, 1999) explores Dryden's translational involvement with Latin. David Norton, *A History of the English Bible as Literature* (Cambridge: CUP, 2000) describes changing attitudes to the language of the King James Bible. On *dragomans* and other go-betweens, see Noel Malcolm, *Agents of Empire: Knights, Corsairs, Jesuits and Spies in the Sixteenth-Century Mediterranean World* (London: Allen Lane, 2015); on Buddhist translation, see Martha P. Y. Cheung (ed.) *An Anthology of Chinese Discourse on Translation*, vol 1: *From the Earliest Times to the Buddhist Project* (Manchester: St Jerome, 2006).

Chapter 2: Definitions

Thought-provoking discussions of the range of translation practices can be found in Theo Hermans, *The Conference of the Tongues* (Manchester: St Jerome, 2007); Douglas Robinson, *The Translator's Turn* (Baltimore and London: Johns Hopkins University Press, 1991); Rita Copeland, *Rhetoric, Hermeneutics and Translation in the Middle Ages: Academic Traditions and Vernacular Texts* (Cambridge: CUP, 1991); Ronit Ricci and Jan van der Putten (eds), *Translation in Asia: Theories, Practices, Histories* (Manchester: St Jerome, 2011); and Sandra Bermann and Catherine Porter (eds), *A Companion to Translation Studies* (Chichester: Wiley-Blackwell, 2014). Useful anthologies are Daniel Weissbort and Astradur

Eysteinsson (eds), *Translation—Theory and Practice: A Historical Reader* (Oxford: OUP, 2006) and Mona Baker (ed.), *Critical Readings in Translation Studies* (Abingdon: Routledge, 2010).

Chapter 3: Words, contexts, and purposes

D. A. Cruse, *Meaning in Language: An Introduction to Semantics and Pragmatics*, 3rd edn (Oxford: OUP, 2011) is a good general account of meaning. J. L. Austin, *How to Do Things With Words* (Oxford: Clarendon Press, 1962) is the classic discussion of speech acts and utterances. Different kinds of equivalence are surveyed in Mona Baker's *In Other Words: A Coursebook on Translation*, 2nd edn (Abingdon: Routledge, 2011). On the role of purpose in translation, see Katharina Reiss and Hans J. Vermeer, *Towards a General Theory of Translational Action: Skopos Theory Explained* (Manchester: St Jerome, 2013). On subtitles and other translation practices in audio-visual media, see Carol O'Sullivan, *Translating Popular Film* (Basingstoke: Palgrave Macmillan, 2010).

Chapter 4: Forms, identities, and interpretations

Otto Neurath, *International Picture Language: The First Rules of Isotype* (London: K. Paul, Trench, Trubner & Co., 1936) is a fascinating introduction to iconic signs. Eric Griffiths and Matthew Reynolds (eds), *Dante in English* (Harmondsworth: Penguin, 2005) gives many examples of translations of Dante. The challenges of translating verse form are entertainingly laid out Douglas R. Hofstadter, *Le Ton Beau de Marot: In Praise of the Music of Language* (London: Bloomsbury, 1997). On interpretive communities, see Stanley Fish, *Is there a Text in this Class: The Authority of Interpretive Communities* (Cambridge, MA, and London: Harvard University Press, 1980) and Samuel Weber, *Institution and Interpretation*, expanded edn (Stanford, CA: Stanford University Press, 2002).

Chapter 5: Power, religion, and choice

Lawrence Venuti, *The Scandals of Translation: Towards an Ethics of Difference* (London and New York: Routledge, 1998) is especially good on the publishing industry. The following books all pursue interesting particular angles, as evidenced by their titles: Eric

Cheyfitz, *The Poetics of Imperialism: Translation and Colonization from* The Tempest *to* Tarzan (New York: OUP, 1991); Sherry Simon, *Gender in Translation: Cultural Identity and the Politics of Transmission* (London: Routledge, 1996); Ziad Elmarsafy, *The Enlightenment Qur'an: The Politics of Translation and the Construction of Islam* (Oxford: Oneworld, 2009); Mona Baker, *Translation and Conflict: A Narrative Account* (London: Routledge, 2006). General discussion can be found in Michael Cronin, *Translation and Identity* (London: Routledge, 2006) and Maria Tymoczko and Edwin Gentzler (eds), *Translation and Power* (Amherst: University of Massachusetts Press, 2002).

Chapter 6: Words in the world

Both the global trade in translations and the logistics of interpretation in the European Parliament are entertainingly surveyed in David Bellos, *Is that a Fish in your Ear: Translation and the Meaning of Everything* (London: Particular Books, 2011). Michael Cronin, *Translation in the Digital Age* (Abingdon: Routledge, 2013) is a thought-provoking discussion. Esperança Bielsa and Susan Bassnett offer a helpful survey in *Translation in Global News* (Abingdon: Routledge, 2009). See also Mona Baker's urgent book *Translating Dissent: Voices from and with the Egyptian Revolution* (Abingdon: Routledge, 2016).

Chapter 7: Translational literature

Tim Parks gives examples of losses in the translation of fiction in *Translating Style: A Literary Approach to Translation; A Translation Approach to Literature*, 2nd edn (Manchester: St Jerome, 2007). Rebecca L. Walkowitz pursues a contrasting line in *Born Translated: The Contemporary Novel in an Age of World Literature* (New York: Columbia University Press, 2015). Peter Robinson's *Poetry and Translation: The Art of the Impossible* (Liverpool: Liverpool University Press, 2010) offers sensitive reflections on its subject. Clive Scott, *Literary Translation and the Rediscovery of Reading* (Cambridge: CUP, 2012) explores translation as a way of displaying readers' responses. See also Matthew Reynolds, *The Poetry of Translation: From Chaucer & Petrarch to Homer & Logue* (Oxford: OUP, 2011).

Publisher's acknowledgements

We are grateful for permission to include the following copyright material in this book.

Extracts from 'Interview: Interpreters in conflict—the view from within', Louise Askew and Myriam Salama Carr, *Translation Studies* (Taylor & Francis, 2011) 4.1, pp. 103–8, reprinted by permission of the publisher (Taylor & Francis Ltd, <http://www.tandfonline.com>).

Extracts from Christine Brooke-Rose, 'Between', in *The Brooke-Rose Omnibus*: *Four Novels- Out, Such, Between, Thru*, 2nd edn (Carcanet Press, 2006).

Extracts from Dorothy L. Sayers (trans.) *Dante: The Divine Comedy*, Vol. 1: *Hell* (Penguin, 1949).

Extracts from 'Song of the Bowmen of Shu' and 'The Beautiful Toilet' By Ezra Pound, from PERSONAE, copyright ©1926 by Ezra Pound. Reprinted by permission of New Directions Publishing Corp, and Faber and Faber Ltd.

Extracts from Rabia Rehmen, 'Translator', in Kate Clanchy (ed.), *The Path: An Anthology by the First Story Group at Oxford Spires Academy* (London: First Story Limited, 2015). By permission.

Extracts from <www.valentinagosetti.wordpress.com/>.

Translation

Index

ONLINE CATALOGUE
A Very Short Introduction

Our online catalogue is designed to make it easy to find your ideal Very Short Introduction. View the entire collection by subject area, watch author videos, read sample chapters, and download reading guides.

http://global.oup.com/uk/academic/general/vsi_list/

SOCIAL MEDIA
Very Short Introduction

Join our community
www.oup.com/vsi

- Join us online at the official Very Short Introductions **Facebook** page.
- Access the thoughts and musings of our authors with our online **blog**.
- Sign up for our monthly **e-newsletter** to receive information on all new titles publishing that month.
- Browse the full range of Very Short Introductions online.
- Read **extracts** from the Introductions for free.
- If you are a teacher or lecturer you can order inspection copies quickly and simply via our website.